BLOOD, SWEAT AND FEARS

Robert D. Garcia

authorHOUSE®

AuthorHouse™
1663 Liberty Drive
Bloomington, IN 47403
www.authorhouse.com
Phone: 1 (800) 839-8640

Published by AuthorHouse 08/26/2016

ISBN: 978-1-5246-2648-8 (sc)
ISBN: 978-1-5246-2646-4 (hc)
ISBN: 978-1-5246-2647-1 (e)

Library of Congress Control Number: 2016914034

Print information available on the last page.

The following forward by Janet Johnson SA/FBI (Ret) mentions "Jimmy" in her account of the operation. Jimmy is the undercover name I used throughout my undercover career, as I will mention in the "Undercover Operation's chapter of this book. Janet uses the name "Bob" in the last paragraph of her foreword.

FOREWORD

It was a warm, late summer evening in southeastern New Mexico. Local task force officers and federal agents gathered around a table as the night's operational plan was being briefed. In some respects, it was not unlike many other plans presented around this same table, administrative requirements and logistical details were discussed: everyone had heard them a hundred times before. Then the electricity in the room began to rise and everyone became more focused as the details of this particular operation began to emerge.

"Jimmy," our undercover agent, had recently infiltrated a Phoenix-based drug-trafficking organization that had been supplying illegal narcotics to the local area. While it had not been a long-term investigation, it had certainly been an intense one. "Jimmy" had been in daily contact with the supplier, and his associates, and had acquired an extensive amount of audio-recorded evidence.

Through a nicely planned series of events, "Jimmy" was able to successfully insert himself into the organization. He had already made drug purchases, increasing the amount purchased each time as the supplier's trust had been gained. However, during his last drug purchase, "Jimmy" was unexpectedly "fronted," or provided on credit, an even larger amount of drugs than what had just been purchased. A few days had passed since the "front," and the supplier wanted his money and he wanted it now…threats were already starting to be made.

As the amount of drugs "Jimmy" had obtained through the course of the investigation already merited the highest level of federal prosecution, there were to be no further funds made available by the federal government to pay for the drugs previously provided on credit. A quick plan was put into place and it was now time to make the arrests.

In retrospect, it was really our own fault that we were not able to sustain the investigation any longer. We should have been expecting the unexpected would happen; such was always the way when "Jimmy" was the undercover. It seemed everyone in the drug-trafficking world liked "Jimmy". With his easygoing manner, his cowboy hat and handlebar mustache he looked, walked and talked like a man who was more comfortable around horses than men. Every time "Jimmy" performed as the undercover agent on an operation, we were successful, in some cases like this one, too successful, too quickly.

On this particular operation, I prayed that "Jimmy's" affability would sustain us long enough for us to catch the supplier and his associates off guard and make the arrests without anyone getting hurt. Tonight's plan was for "Jimmy" to meet the Phoenix-based supplier at the local casino. Typically, when there is a lot of money and/or drugs involved, the supplier will have other associates in the area to provide protection. On this night, the supplier did not disappoint.

The risk of danger was always high in this line of work, but the ante was certainly high tonight: we were luring an unknown number of bad guys to a public location, with "Jimmy" inserted in the middle of the operation, to supposedly pay the supplier with money we didn't have. "Jimmy's" delivery of the code word to the arrest teams would have to be flawless in its timing and execution and the arrest team's convergence on his location would have to be precise and exact. What could possibly go wrong?

As the meeting time drew near, the officers and agents checked and rechecked their team assignments, their personal tasking's, and the extraction plans should it become necessary to extract "Jimmy" from a deteriorating situation before, during or after the arrests of the bad guys were made. It was time to roll.

As I sat at my assigned location inside the security office at the casino, I was keenly aware that I was responsible for calling out over the radios all observed activity captured on the casino's video surveillance system. I tried to curb my own growing sense of anticipation, and attempted to nonchalantly converse with my partner about how many times I had been at this very same casino in my official capacity as a federal agent. Not once, in over ten years of working in the area, had I been to the casino for a casual night out with friends. It was always about the work. I wondered if my partner could hear the nervousness in my voice on this particular evening.

I sat silently for a few moments and reflected on the amazing adventures I had been a part of during my time as a federal agent working drug investigations in New Mexico. Every law enforcement agency in southeastern New Mexico worked with reduced manpower, with few resources and often in austere locations. We literally depended on one another for survival. I loved the partnerships we had built over the years. We had taken lot of drugs off the streets, arrested a lot of people, and hopefully made our communities safer for our children.

All of a sudden my introspection was interrupted as we observed the subject's vehicle arrive at the casino, quickly followed by another vehicle. It was show time and the adrenaline started pumping! A short time later, "Jimmy" gave the code word setting forth the chain of events outlined in the operational plan. The supplier and his associates were arrested and all the good guys, including "Jimmy," returned safely home to their families that night.

"Jimmy" is officially retired now, but his legend continues. Bob, you are one of the most honorable men I have ever met and it was my privilege and honor to have worked alongside you those years in New Mexico. Stay safe my friend and May God Bless!

Janet L. Johnson
SA/FBI

For the brave men and women who have served, or are still serving this great nation.

For the brave men and women who are serving in a law enforcement capacity, may the Lord continue to bless and keep you safe

For the International Police colleagues I have had the honor and privilege of meeting and serving with.

To the Vietnam Veterans, Welcome home

Introduction

This collection of stories will take you throughout the course of my military and law enforcement career. A little insight on what it was for me as a Marine and police officer. Within the course of my life events, I have encountered situations that would have one believe me to be insane for doing the things I did. This book will take you through the phases of my career focusing particularly on my experience as an undercover narcotics agent.

I am in no way pretending to be any kind of a hero or an expert in anything. I write for entertainment, to bring a smile to the reader. Personally, the true heroes are the men and women in military uniform, because of their commitment to duty that never made it home or have left a part of them on some foreign land. I have experienced combat, been shot at and had guns pointed at my head during my duties as a Marine, law enforcement officer, undercover agent and a police contractor. I have never considered myself as a hero. I felt it was my duty to serve and do what little I could for my country.

In the sixties and seventies, many service men and women returned from Vietnam to a different America. Many arrived to protest as soon as they stepped on American soil. I experienced this first hand. Today, I am glad the majority of the American people have taken a different approach to our returning service men and women. To this day, whenever I meet a Vietnam Veteran, I will walk up to them, shake their hand and welcome them home.

It is my intention to write about humorous incidents that have occurred while serving in uniform. At this point I kind of wish I had one of my former police supervisors with their yellow hi-lighter or red ink pen to check my spelling and grammar. Some of the incidents I write about may seem graphic or uncaring. It is a part of what we in law enforcement or military had to contend with on a daily basis.

I have lived off of adrenaline for as long as I can remember. I relished the rush I would experience after some traumatic event I voluntarily put myself through. I guess this all began when I started riding bareback broncs in the military rodeo circuit. I loved that adrenaline rush I got. In most of my career, I would volunteer for anything that would provide me with the same type of adrenaline rush.

The contents of this manuscript are based on memory, field notes and police reports that I currently am in possession of. For legal reasons and the purpose of this book, names and locations of incidents have been changed or omitted. In the undercover section of this book, much data is omitted due to pending court cases. As law enforcement officers we are trained to take field notes whenever possible. Field notes were essential when going on a call. They were used to refresh your memory when writing reports. After leaving law enforcement, I kept most of my notes, as I am sure many law enforcement officers do.

I enlisted in the US Marine Corps at age 17, a skinny kid barely weighing 130 pounds. I dropped out of our local high school midway through the 10th grade. I was not doing well in any of my classes, and the Vietnam War was near its end. My two older brothers Eddy and Joe were both serving in Vietnam and I looked forward to serving my country as well.

I actually left school and walked across town to the Marine recruiting office. I told the recruiter of my intention on enlisting. After asking my age, the recruiter told me I would have to have one of my parent's signatures. Eventually my mother agreed and signed. Shortly thereafter, I was off to seek new adventures. I was sent to Marine Corps Recruiting Depot (MCRD) San Diego for boot camp.

CHAPTER I

USMC
Uncle Sam's Misguided Children

US Marine Corps General Orders

- To take charge of this post and all government property in view

- To walk my post in a military manner, keeping always on the alert and observing everything that takes place within sight and hearing

- To report all violations of orders I am instructed to enforce

- To repeat all calls from post more distance from the guardhouse than my own

- To quit my post only when properly relieved

- To receive, obey and pass on to the century who relieves me all orders from the commanding officer, officer of the day, and officers and noncommissioned officers of the guard only.

- To talk to no one except in the line of duty

- To give the alarm in case of fire or disorder

- To call the corporal of the guard in any case not covered by instructions

- To salute all officers and all colors and standards not cased

- To be especially watchful, and during the time for challenging, to challenge all persons on or near my post and to allow no one to pass without proper authority

  Note: each of these had to be memorized word for word during boot camp. I still can recite most of them.

MCRD San Diego

The United States Marine Corps, known as the world's greatest fighting force has, two training regiments (boot camps), one at Marine Corp Recruiting Depot (MCRD) San Diego, California which is located adjacent to the San Diego airport. The other location is at MCRD Paris Island South Carolina, which host the women Marine boot camp as well. It is common practice for anyone living east of the Mississippi river, to be sent to Paris Island and those living west of the Mississippi are sent to San Diego for training.

Before one can call themselves a Marine, a recruit must successfully complete the entire training program at one of the two Marine Corps Recruiting Depots. At the time, the program was eleven weeks and it is my understanding, it is now thirteen weeks. Recruits that are dropped from the training cycle were either dropped for medical or personal reasons. They were sent to medical platoons for rehab, motivation platoon, or to what at the time was call the fat farm. It appeared no one just got out of the Corps.

I was shipped off to MCRD San Diego, CA. The Marine Corps for reasons unknown to me seems to like all their recruits to arrive in the middle of the night. We arrived at boot camp on a bus that had picked us up at the San Diego airport. As soon as it stopped at MCRD, a maniac Drill Instructor, wearing a smoky bear hat and tailored uniform, boarded the bus and began screaming orders on what "his Marine Corps" expected us, newly arrived boots (recruits), to do. I did not understand most of what he said, but followed every recruit off the bus. We were directed to stand on yellow foot prints that were painted on the grinder or parade deck (asphalt). The painted foot prints were in a forty five degree angle so when the recruits stood on them their feet were already in a forty five degree angle with the heels touching. At that point the recruits were in shock and confused, I included.

We were given further instructions by several irate Drill Instructors who were jumping around us bellowing orders. Making us shout (at the top of our lungs) "Sir yes Sir" and "Aye Aye Sir". We marched to another building for haircuts. During the so called march to get haircuts, all were then made to lock our arms with the recruits next to us. The Drill Instructor would shout (count cadence) "Left Right Left" and we had better be in step. I recall thinking that it was funny we had to lock our arm with each other like little school girls. I must of said something to the recruit next to me in a low voice, almost a whisper. One of the Drill Instructors heard me and pounced on me. It didn't take long to realize these drill instructors could hear a humming bird fart. I was made to get on my face, in the push up position for what seemed like an eternity until it was my turn to get my hair cut. After that, the rest of the late night was a blur.

We were moved to different locations; for uniform issue, get rid of contraband, medical and MOS *Military Occupational Specialty* that characterizes the type of work you will be assigned too after boot camp testing. All that and much more took place in a matter of days. By the end of each day, we were hoarse from too much shouting.

Expecting the worse, I went in with the understanding that I was going to get my ass kicked or even killed in boot camp. It was believed by many that Marine Drill Instructors could beat you into submission. However, that was not the case and the DI's could find them in a lot of trouble. Many recruits, including yours truly, were taken into the DI's hut and "secretly" paid for our mistakes. The first time I was ordered to the DI's hut along with another recruit, for some reason I do not remember, we were made to hang on a wall locker with only our elbows. I cannot say how long we were left to hang there but after that both of us, being squad leaders at the time, made sure our squads did as they were told. I later was fired from the squad leader position Thank god. As I am writing this my son Patrick is getting ready to go to boot camp in a matter of weeks.

Boot Camp is divided into 3 phases: phase I is the initial phase where recruits are issued uniforms, learn marching drills, Marine Corps history and lots of Physical Training (PT); Phase II consist of rifle qualification and more PT; Phase III final inspection, marching drills, getting ready for graduation and more PT. We began phase I with eighty recruits. Towards the end of phase 3 we were down to 45-50 recruits. I learned to keep my mouth shut and tried my best to not make myself noticeable. For some reason, that didn't always work for me.

United States Marine Corps Dill Instructors have a mission to break down new recruits. Breaking down the recruits sense of self and selfishness, and rebuild them into highly trained fighters. It is referred to as "Making Marines". With that being said, the way they do that at times may seem comical if you are watching from the outside. They have always had a way with words, having their own vocabulary. The following are but a few of their own artistic form of quotes used during my days in boot camp.

While marching and the platoon is looking "raggedy" our Drill Instructor would shout "Hippity hop, mob stop, just stop". "Get on your faces ladies" meaning in the push up position.

If one was taking his time completing a task; "Oh! Any day sweet heart".

"I will PT you until your eye balls roll out of your head".

"Bends and thrust until I get tired".

During the week when the platoon would mess up and the Drill instructor knew he would be on duty the following Sunday he would say "Don't worry bitch, I will have you all day Sunday". "You WILL pay". Sundays were still considered training days but we were allowed to attend Sunday Morning Worship Services, spit shine our leather gear or study our knowledge books. The DI on duty always remembered we "owed him one" so he would send us out to the pits. We never looked forward to Sundays. I soon became a constant visitor to "the pit".

For some reason it became customary to hear the DI bellow "Private Garcia, come here worm". He would grab me from the throat and choke me. They had a way of grabbing one around the esophagus with their fingers and applying just enough pressure to make you think about the mistakes in your life. I guess they were fond of me. I have been accused of being a communist plot sent in by the communist to mess up the Drill Instructor's Marine Corps.

One of my favorite cadences the Drill Instructor would make us sing during our daily runs;

Little bitty birdie with the yellow bill (we had to repeat)

Landed on my window sill

I lured him in with a piece of bread

Then I crushed its F***ing head

Phase I

After the first 3-4 days at MCRD, on a Friday known as 'Black Friday", we are introduced to OUR Drill Instructors, These drill instructors were the ones we got to spend the next eleven weeks in hell with.

One memorable day, during a 'junk-on-the-bunk' inspection, with the entire platoon standing in front of our individual racks (beds, for you civilian), we had to display our entire military issued gear and clothing neatly folded and placed on top of our racks. Everything had to be in its place and no article of clothing would have any 'Irish Pennants'. Irish Pennants are pieces of threads sticking out of the clothing article or on Marine covers (again, for you civilian, hats or caps). During the inspection, one of the Drill Instructor was inspecting the recruit standing to my right. Apparently he found Irish pennants on the recruit's covers; he began stacking all the covers on the recruits head. I glanced out the corner of my eye and saw this recruit with about 5 or 6 covers stacked on his head. Before catching myself, I smirked out loud. Like buzzards on a gut wagon, I had 3 Drill Instructors circling me shouting all kinds of threats. After the inspection, the entire platoon was sent to the pits to roll in the sand while Drill Instructor Sgt. Corpus (not real name) wet us down with a water hose.

Fully covered with sand, we were then marched to the parade deck made to roll on the hot grinder (asphalt) while the DI shouted, "bake my sugar cookies". The platoon was instructed to shout out "thank you Private Garcia". It's a wonder the platoon didn't give me a blanket party. For those that don't know and if you have ever watched Full Metal Jacket, a blanket party is when the recruits catch you in bed, wrap a blanket on you and hold it down so tight you cannot move. The recruits then beat you with bars of soap in side of socks so as to not leave any marks. In the movie they gave Private Pyle a blanket party. Like I said, I was lucky not to get one throughout my time in boot camp as I kept messing up causing the platoon to do extra PT.

•

Often while we were being doused with water by the Senior Drill Instructor, for some mistake someone had made, he would recite his version on how Marines came into existent. *"Marines come from the sea. We are the spawn of Poseidon. We left the sea and crawled up the beach into existence", therefore we are amphibian and love the water".* (You will see this again readers) All the while he is dousing us with a water hose on a cool evening. I didn't dare make any snide remarks then.

I will add each platoon is assigned 3 drill instructors; the senior DI or "The Hat" is of higher rank.

•

Drill Instructors had a way of making one laugh if one would dare. They had their own vocabulary anytime they open their mouths. According to the drill instructors, every Marine was one color. There is no white, black, brown, yellow, or any color in the rainbow. There were only green Marines or dark green Marines, but everyone was green and equally worthless.

What little down time we had between training, we were given the order to 'study your knowledge'. Our knowledge books was the 'Guide Books for Marines'. It contained everything you needed to know about the Marine Corps. From the way the uniform, with ribbons and badges was worn to

Marine Corps History. We had to memorize our eleven General Orders and most everything in the book. Upon being asked of any subject in the 'knowledge book' we had better recite it word for word. If we did not know or remember it we had to say "Sir the private was instructed but the private forgot Sir". Of course we paid for that as well.

We were forbidden to use the word 'you' or 'I'. If we addressed the drill instructor (you better have a good reason too) you would have to 'request permission to speak to the Drill Instructor'. If you talked about yourself you would say 'the private'. The reason for this was to create unity. I once made the mistake of using "I" and got poked in the eye by the DI who reminded me what "I" was.

Phase II Rifle Range

For the second phase of Boot Camp, we are sent to MCB (Marine Corp Base for you uninitiated) Camp Pendleton California, for 2 weeks of firearms training. The first week is for working the Butts (pulling targets) and rifle familiarization. It is called Snapping In. At the time we are issued the M14 rifle and after graduation we were issued the much lighter M16 rifle.

The second week was the actual firing and qualification with our weapon. I found the M14 to be a very accurate weapon. We shot our weapons from the 200, 300 and 500 yard line using the weapon's sights only. We each had to recite the M14 as being air cooled, magazine fed, and gas operated, 7.62 mm shoulder weapon.

During the weapons phase, the Drill Instructors were not as harsh on us so as to let us concentrate on passing the rifle qualification. Unless someone messed up severely. This time it was not yours truly; one of our Drill Instructor's (no names mentioned here) marched us to "the pit" with our recently cleaned rifle. He made us lie in the prone position (face down) in the hot sand with our arms and our M14 straight out in front of us. The Drill Instructor ordered us to place the butt of the rifle on the deck (ground) with the barrel straight up in the air. Upon his command, we were to push up and the only part to touch the ground was the butt of the rifle and the toes of our boots.

Everyone one of us were straining to keep the rest of our bodies from touching the ground. I recall all the muscles in my body burning as I strained to keep from touching that hot sand. Although it would last only a few seconds it seemed like an eternity. We did it over and over until the Drill Instructor got bored. For me, this was one of the hardest punishments I ever got in boot camp. Did I say punishment? The Drill Instructors did not think of this as punishment. They always justified it by saying "the more you sweat in peace, the less you bleed in war" or "one day this will save your life".

Much like our daily "thump calls", a Drill Instructor (again no names here) would instruct us to "get on the road for thump call". As a platoon we would rush out side and get into formation. The command of "parade rest" was given and we would stand with our hands behind our backs, our feet spread slightly apart. The Drill instructor would walk up to each of us and say "one day this will save your life" and punch us in the stomach. After a few thump call days we were getting used to it and the thumping ceased. Towards the end of Boot Camp we felt confidence (or brainwashed) and there was virtually no physical demand or task we could not accomplish.

Phase III

We ended 3rd phase by completing our final inspections, final drill and required Physical Fitness Test (PFT). As part of Platoon 1028 I graduated as a United States Marine.

As part of our training cycle we attended Marine Corps History classes. A great emphasis was placed on General Lewis "Chesty" Puller. General Puller was fondly known as Chesty Puller by Marines. He served in the Marine Corps from 1918 to 1955 and retired with the rank of Lt General. Chesty literally came up through the ranks beginning as a private and shortly after went to Officer Candidate School (OCS – I prefer to call it Organize Chicken Shit). He served in several campaigns starting with the

Banana Wars, WWII and Korea. Puller always placed the enlisted men's needs before his own or his officers. Therefore he was loved buy all. He was known to step on toes and was not afraid of offending the top brass at the Pentagon. As part of our prayer session before "lights out", as a platoon, we would say "Good night Chesty where ever you are".

I did meet Drill Instructor Sgt. Corpus (not real name) back in 1993 when I was a police officer in the South Texas border town of Hidalgo. I happened to be in my office which was near the front desk and lobby. I overheard the receptionist talking to a gentleman that had come in.

I overheard the gentleman mentioned something about being a bounty hunter and was on his way to Mexico to bring back a fugitive. The receptionist asked for his name he answered 'Corpus'. I remembered thinking, "Corpus', I know that name". I went to the front of the lobby and immediately recognized this short, stalky, spawn of Satan. I went up to him and said "Sergeant Corpus". I could tell by his reaction that his 'brain housing group' (Marine terminology for he was thinking), was working overtime trying to place me. I mentioned to him "Platoon 1028, 1st Battalion, Alpha Company 1972". Letting his guard down, he came up and gave me a hug.

I still addressed him as Sergeant Corpus, either out of fear or respect. We became good friends. He and his wife were both bounty hunters and lived nearby. They would often visit my wife and me. On one occasion, I invited Sergeant Corpus to a local saloon located outside of the city. This place was a local watering hole where bikers, DEA, police and farmers would hang out. As we walked in, several of the DEA agents in the bar saw Sergeant Corpus and greeted him. They knew who he was. Apparently he had done some work for them, bringing in some of their wanted persons. I've since lost track of Drill Instructor, Spawn of Satan, Sgt Corpus. Semper Fi.

Amtracs: Uncle Sam's Misguided Children (USMC)

Upon leaving boot camp, I was transferred to Schools Battalion where I was given the MOS (Military Occupational Specialty) 1833 Amphibian

Tractor Crewman. We were known as an Amtracker or tractor rat. The Amtrac (LVTP7) is an amphibian assault vehicle with tank tracks that can maneuver both in water and on land. The tracked vehicle was developed to carry up to 25 combat loaded Marines. The Marines could be loaded from a ship and transport anywhere on land. In the water the LVTP7 was operated by water jets with a speed of up to 12 knots. On land it was powered by 500 HP Detroit diesel engines with the maximum speed of 55 mph. I loved driving these vehicles. Each tractor consisted of a Crew Chief, Gunner, Driver and Crewman. The crewman normally sat in the cargo area of the vehicle.

After Schools Battalion in Southern California, I was transferred to 2nd Amtrac Battalion, 2nd Marine Division, Camp Lejeune NC. My orders were to report to Alpha Company, 2nd Platoon. It was there where I met Platoon Gunnery Sergeant Epp an old salty Vietnam veteran. The Gunny as we so fondly called him, was probably in his mid-30s. Years later when I watched the Clint Eastwood movie Heartbreak Ridge, the main character Gunny Tom Highway reminded me of Gunny Epp, cigar and all. 2nd Platoon at the time consisted mostly of returning Vietnam vets. The rest of us were just 17 and 18 year old privates. Under the care and mentorship of the veterans we had our butts kicked and quickly learned the ropes on being a proper Tractor Rat. Right outside the back gate of Courthouse Bay where 2nd Amtracs was located, stood a bar that catered to Amtracs and 2nd Force Recon Marines. 2nd Force Recon was located near 2nd Amtrac BN on Onslo Beach. Amtracs and Recon always got along well for some unknown reason. Perhaps it was because we were looked down upon by the regular Marine grunts. Within our amtracs we drove anywhere and could carry our own recreational beverages in hidden compartments inside our amtrac which was shared with Force Recon Marines. Life was good as a tractor rat.

We later participated in various operations as a platoon in Cyprus and Lebanon. On this "Mediterranean float" as it was called, several of the countries we visited were relieved after we had left. At the end of my tour with 2nd Amtracs, I was deployed to the 1st Amtrac Battalion 3rd Marine Division in Okinawa Japan. It was there where I finally attended and completed high school sponsored by the base. While assigned to

H&S Company (we preferred to call it Hide and Slide) we participated in operations in the Philippines and Vietnam. I will save that for a later book.

While station on Okinawa we were on a float (cruise) with Battalion Landing Team 3/4 (BLT3/4). These floats or cruises are 6 month deployments aboard a ship with the Navy to respond anywhere our Commander In Chief need us to quell any hate and discontent around the world. As part of Operation Frequent Wind in 1975 during the evacuations of Vietnam, our Amtrac platoon was deployed on the USS Peoria LST 1183. After the fall of Saigon and the last American personnel were evacuated from the US Embassy in Saigon, our ship made a port-of-call in Hong Kong. Meaning all the drinks and women we could take in the few short days in port. I'll try to keep it clean here dear readers. Shortly thereafter we returned to Okinawa.

•

My best friends and brother Marines who for the life of me I do not understand and our good fortune, happened to get station in the same platoons in our first 4 years in the 'Crotch' (Corps). My good friends and buddies, J B, JB was a tall southern Californian beach goer who resembled Tom Selleck in his younger days, The Hat, was short for Hatfield who was a descendant of the Hatfield's of the Hatfield's and McCoy fame and there was RLB who as a former oil field worker and was always ready for a good fight. We always seemed to get deployed to the same location. Fortunately for us but unfortunate for the world. Somehow "Private Mischief" (a.k.a. Murphy of Murphy's Law fame, remember that name you will see it again), would always get the same transfer orders and follow us everywhere we went.

In Hong Kong, we were enjoying some of the local wild life and recreational beverages. The Cinderella clock struck midnight and we had to get back to the ship. We somehow made it to the pier to wait for the Navy liberty boats. These boats were to pick us up and return us to our ship, docked out in the harbor. As we waited for the liberty boats, my friend Jim said something about us being Amtrackers and it meant we were Amphibians so we should swim to the ship anchored quite distant from the pier. Well readers being Marines and our Marine Corps anthem has Air, Land and Sea in its lyrics. SEA meant water and we were Amphibians, we took off our shoes and dove into the dark, dirty water of the Hong Kong harbor. We probably swam about 500 yards before the US Navy Shore Patrol pulled us out of the water. We were taken before the Navy's Chief Master at Arms (CMA, the ships police chief) who then turned us over to our First Sergeant. The First Sergeant, lovingly looked at us as the CMA read to us from the 'the good book' and told our First Sergeant what we had done. During this time we were still at attention, wet and shaking. I believed we shook more out of fear of the First Sergeant than our cold wet clothing. As punishment we were restricted to the ship and not allowed to go on 'liberty call' the next couple of days. Oh well. Semper Fi.

I recall JB and I swimming in the dirty canals of Venice Italy while we were with BLT 2/6 back in 1973. Private Mischief came along for the ride on that float as well.

•

As a platoon we were also deployed to the Philippines to train with the Philippine Marines and assist in searching for insurgents that had been terrorizing the locals in the villages of Tacloban and Bacolod. During our down time we were sent to the Jungle Environmental Survival School (JEST) on the island of Negros. The Marine Corps again decides we needed to stay wet. We had water survival training in the shark infested waters off the Philippine coast, in the South China Sea. As part of that training we had to be in full utilities (MC speak for work uniform) and combat boots. We removed our boots while bobbing in the water, tied them together and hung them around our necks. We were dropped off about 1000 yards off the coast and had to swim to a designated spot on shore. Non swimmers were included in this training. The non-swimmers wore an inflatable life vest called a 'May West' and swimmers had to help the non-swimmers in as well. I was assigned a "swim buddy" who happened to be a non-swimmer. Roy (not his real name) was that swim buddy. I was fighting the current and trying to maintain alignment with the beach landing zone. Every time a wave would hit Roy's face he would panic and freeze up on me. After a while the safety boat pulled up alongside of us and

I thought, great, we don't have to make it all the way. I was wrong. Roy was picked up by the crew of the safety boat and I was told to continue swimming. I will say, trying to swim fully clothed and fighting a strong current that was taking us out to the sea was not a fun task. Being Marines and children of Poseidon we overcame that obstacle and made it to shore.

•

As mentioned above, we were volunteered to attend the Jungle Environmental Survival Training school (JEST). JEST school involved attending class room instructions and then out into the jungle divided into groups of twos with only a bag of rice and our K-Bar knife (look it up). We were to apply what we had learned in the classroom setting, taught to us by the Philippines Negritos. The Negritos, as they are called, are Indigenous people of that area of the Philippines and are noted jungle survival and tracking experts. JB was my partner and so we set out into the jungle for some more fun and adventure. After a couple of days of not eating very well, we found ourselves eating everything we could catch slithering, crawling or flying. We turned to sleeping high up in the trees as cobras were frequently seen. Someone forgot to tell us that cobras were known to climb trees as well. All in all we survived and had a great time. We did worry about being kidnapped by the Islamic insurgents that were on the island. They probably would have turned us loose if they had to feed us.

•

While deployed to the US Navy Base, Subic Bay Philippines, we are given a safety course on what not to do and place to avoid. At the time, Philippines insurgents known as the Moro National Liberation Front (MNLF) were known to kidnap American service personnel and hold them for ransom.

One afternoon after completing my daily duties, my partners in crime and I made plans to meet at a local hangout in the city of Olongapo. I was running late and told my fellow Marines I would be late and would meet them in the city.

As I walked out the main gate of Subic Bay US Naval Base, I was approached by a Philippine young man who I recognized as working in our part of the base shining shoes and boots. He had called me by name and asked where I was going. I told him I was going to meet the guys at the bar. He asked if I recognized him and I said I did. He then asked if he could join us at the bar and I told him it was his choice and his country. As we were crossing 'Shit River' (those that have been there know what I mean) he asked if we could stop by his flat (house) for a minute to pick up something. I thought, what the hell, and said only for a minutes. We walked through back alleys in a winding, cluttered city. We arrived at a small house in a cluttered neighborhood. I was invited into the home. When I walked in, I saw several men sitting at a table playing cards. I was introduced to a large man sitting at the poker table who claimed to be the uncle. By that time, red flags or spider senses began going off in my head, especially when the large man told me his name was Ali or some shit like that. The majority of the Filipinos I knew had Spanish surnames. This one, I recall had a Muslim name. The kid who invited me there had gone into another room and I had not seen him since. I was invited to sit and play poker and first I declined. I was at the same time scanning the room and trying to remain calm. I noticed there were no women or children in the room and counted five Filipino men in the room with me. I recall thinking I did not want to make it obvious I knew I may be in trouble. The room itself appeared to sit in the back of a house. There was a closed door to my right that appeared to be another room. One of the men was wearing a camouflage shirt happened to stroll to the only exit door and stood by it thus blocking my exit. Red flags and spider senses started going off in my head. I fought hard to remain calm. I sat myself at the table with a wall to my back where I could keep everyone in sight as well as the closed door to my right. I asked where "the Kid" went too and was told to don't worry he will be back. It seemed like everyone was trying to be extra friendly. The "uncle" asked if I spoke Spanish and I replied in Spanish that I was fluent. The "uncle" said he spoke Spanish as well. I began conversation in Spanish trying to get then off their guard until I could figure a safe way out of this predicament.

While sitting at the table, cards were dealt to me. I continued scanning the room, talking and listening for any noise coming from the room on my right. I then heard noise coming from that very same room. I kept talking and appearing to be relaxed. There was a pack of cigarettes and matches on the table and asked if I could have one. I did not smoke at the time, but I had come up with a plan. The man with the Camo shirt was still standing by the exit door. I planned on going through him and the door if things went south.

I struck the match as if I was going to lite the cigarette and held it in my hand. Meanwhile I kept talking and would not shut up. I notice "Uncle Ali" was looking at the lit match as if to see my dumb ass was about to burn my fingers. I felt the flames reach the tip of my fingers and I shouted, threw the match down. Catching everyone off guard, I then shoved the table towards Uncle Ali as hard as I could. I jumped over half of it and plowed my way through "Camo shirt" standing by the door. On my way out, I caught a glimpse of someone coming out of the room that was on my right. I hit the back alley and started running. Because of the winding alleyway I did not see anyone chasing me nor did I want to wait and find out. I made it back to the base where I reported the incident.

●

While I was on Okinawa, I got to visit my sister Diana and her husband Jim. My brother-in-law Jim was in the US Army, based at Torii Station. On weekends, I would visit them and get invited to the base club. Being the only US Marine in the club, I was treated very well.

●

After departing Okinawa, I returned to the states and sent to 3rd Amtracs, 1st Mar Div in Camp Pendleton California. Camp Del Mar was home to 3rd Amtracs. My same Marine brothers along with Private Mischief (remember him) were assigned together in the southern California base. As usual Amtrac battalions were always located next to a beach. It seemed that the Marine Corps enjoyed keeping us wet as much as we enjoyed being on the beach tanning and entertaining the local wildlife. At times Private

Mischief would invite himself to join us and we wind up in front of the Company 1st Sergeant, blamed for something someone else did.

One such occasion that comes to mind. My friends and I were out in the city of Oceanside California socializing and drinking our favorite beverage. Someone (not me this time) had some trouble with one of the local citizens and the police were called. Private Mischief decided to join us as well, uninvited mind you. Anyway police arrived and the bar owner wanted someone to pay for some chairs that had been broken. The local police accompanied by the Marine Military Police, arrived and handcuffed two of our mates. The rest of us were told to go back to the base. One of us not handcuffed, decided to speak out and demanded the police let our mates go. Well gentile readers, the rest of us got hauled off to the city lockup as well. I should of learned to keep my mouth shut.

Early the following morning, we were expecting and dreading the company 1st Sergeant to pick us up from the city jail, but instead, the Battalion Sergeant Major showed up. The Sergeant Major in question was none other than Sgt. Major Valdez. The last Marine to leave the Embassy in Vietnam during the fall of Saigon in April 1975 under Operation Frequent Wind. The Sergeant Major who happened to be our Battalion Sgt. Major was allowed to take us out and escort us back to the base.

I will not go into detail about our punishments but we had a lot of respect for Sgt. Major Valdez.

The Marine Corps in its infinite wisdom decided to separate us shortly after. Cpl. RLB and I (a Corporal as well) were transferred to a platoon that was made up of mostly new recruits. Cpl. RLB and I were the only ones with any type of experience since we had previously been deployed overseas. The platoon Commander was a young Lieutenant (butter bars) who had been a math teacher in civilian life. Lieutenant Ski is what we called him. He was your typical nerd looking, glasses wearing "boot" lieutenant. He really tried with us.

One morning during formation, Cpl. RLB was standing in front of me as first squad leader and I was the second squad leader. The Lieutenant (LT) was conducting a rifle inspection on the entire platoon. He began with Cpl. RLB. When the lieutenant stopped in front of Cpl. RLB, RLB brought his rifle up to 'port arms' in the way of a fancy drill team movement. He kicked the butt of his M16 rifle while it was resting on the deck (ground for you civilians) with the heel of his right foot, made it spin and brought it to port arms, including unlocking the bolt with the charging handle. The LT said "*Cpl. RLB that is not the way you do inspection arms. You are here to teach these new Marines the correct way*". Cpl. RLB responded "*that is the way I was taught sir*". I was trying not to laugh because I knew that RLB was only messing with this new boot lieutenant. "*Cpl. RLB, I want you to make an about face (turn around) and let Cpl. Garcia (moi) show you the proper way of doing inspection arms*". "*Cpl. Garcia, show Cpl. RLB the proper way of inspection arms*". "*Aye Aye Sir*" I said. I performed the same movement that Cpl. Brown did, keeping a straight face. The rest of the platoon broke out into laughter. The Lieutenant didn't know what to do and only shook his head. "*Platoon dismiss*" the Lieutenant followed that by saying "*Corporal RLB and Corporal Garcia to my office NOW*".

Later RLB and I with the help of the sergeants did get the platoon into shape and we did a short deployment to Alaska for some cold weather training. Again we were wet and cold.

•

After the first four years of active duty in the Corps, I re-enlisted as a Marine reservist stationed at Naval Air Station, Dallas Texas as an Armorer or weapons repairman with Delta Battery 2/14. We would spend all day in the Armory working on weapons. After 2 years, I transferred to the 4th Air Wing MAG 41 at NAS Dallas. It was there I held the billet as a Military Police officer.

Marines have a saying, Once a Marine, Always a Marine. I find that to be true in many ways. Sometimes it affects your children as well.

Years later while on an overseas contract, I went home on leave to had children I was doing contract work overseas. I went home on leave to spend time with my wife and kids. My son Patrick was about 4 years old at the time. As a family we attended church one Sunday morning. After the services we decided to have lunch at a local steak house. The church pastor and his wife had joined us as well.

We were all sitting having a quiet lunch when my son Patrick, stood up on his chair and shouts 'Semper Fi'. He gets off the chair, lays on the floor next to me and commences to do sit ups. Everyone in the restaurant is looking at him. My wife who is sitting across from me is glaring at me like "he's your son, do something". I turned to my son who is still doing sit ups and said "oorah son" and I continued with my meal.

CHAPTER II

Law Enforcement

DALLAS COUNTY SHERIFF'S DEPARTMENT

In early 1980, I began my law enforcement career with the Dallas County Sheriff's Department in Dallas Texas. I had just gotten separated from the Marine Corps active duty status and I reenlisted with a reserve unit of the US Marine Corps. At the time I had been working as a Landscaper and decided to become a police officer. While I was stationed at the Naval Air Station in Grand Prairie Texas, I held the billet (MOS) as a Military Police officer on the base. It was during that time I had the occasion to meet with several local law enforcement officials. It was then that I decided to try my hand in law enforcement.

I applied and got accepted with the Dallas County Sheriff's Department, as a Deputy Sheriff. My first year as a deputy, I was assigned to the detention center located on the top floors of the county court house on Commerce Street in the Dallas city center. After a year I was transferred to the Identification (ID) section of the department. I was trained as an ID technician. My job was to search and classify fingerprints. At that time we did not have the high tech fingerprint scanners that are in use today. All fingerprints had to be classified manually. We had a rather large office with several deputies and clerks working as ID techs. File cabinets with fingerprints card took up most of the office space. Every prisoner that ever came into the system, it was our job to classify the fingerprint cards and manually search existing cards on file to properly identify each person. We were also certified to testify in court on suspect's fingerprints. It was an interesting job.

•

On each desk in the Identification office we had CRT (Cathode Ray Tubes) computers that are now superseded by the modern LCD and plasma computers. In the 1980's these were the top of the line. We had

23

access to the National Criminal Information Center/Texas Criminal Information Center NCIC/TCIC and could send teletype messages state wide. Often times we would receive weather bulletins from the National Weather Service (NWS).

In our office we had several civilian clerks working with us. They too had their own desks with computers. One of our clerks was an older lady who was constantly getting overly excited about anything that came across the teletype, relaying messages from the NWS. I decided, or I should say we, to play a joke on this poor lady one day. Between this other officer (who I will call Albert) and I, we came up with a fake weather bulleting from the National Weather Service in Weatherford Texas. The bulleting we devised announced a Snow Storm Warning is in Effect for Parts of North Texas Including Dallas County. This was the month of July and the temperature was in the upper 90s. Albert and I made the bulletin look official with all the proper wording. From our CRT we could send messages from desk to desk, within the Sheriff's Office or state wide. When the bulletin was ready, I thought I press the desk to desk button on the keyboard to send it to the older clerk's desk computer. Albert and I waited for the message to appear on her screen. She received it and immediately made a copy and ran around the office. She was really excited and was announcing to everyone that could hear, it was going to snow. Albert and I were sitting back proud of our work and were having a good laugh, until the phones started ringing. I was immediately called to the Major's office upstairs.

The major (ID Commander) handed me an official looking bulleting and ask "did you do this". My heart sank immediately. I replied "yes sir I did, but I just sent it to." he quickly interrupted me and said "you idiot, you sent it state wide and we are getting phone calls from all over including TCIC and NCIC". We will be lucky to not have to shut down our computers". After having my ass chewed for about a half hour, I could have sworn, I detected a grin on his face, he told me to go back to work. I returned to the ID office and everyone in there glared at me including the clerk it was meant for. Albert would not look at me, either because he was probably embarrassed for not being called into the commander's office or because he didn't want to laugh.

McAllen Police Department

After leaving the Dallas County Sheriff's Department, I went to work at the McAllen Police Department in the south Texas border town of McAllen. Because of my fingerprint identification background, I went straight into the crime scene division as a fingerprint tech and crime scene search officer. I later had to attend the McAllen Police Academy although I was already a certified police officer. It was no big deal, I enjoyed that as well.

After a stint on patrol, I made a decision to go to college and so I moved to Virginia where I applied at Hampton University Police Department in Hampton Virginia where I can attend school and work as a campus police officer.

Tidewater Regional Police Academy, Hampton Virgina

Attending Hampton University in Hampton Virginia, I was worked as a Campus Police Officer. After my first year with HUPD I was sent to the Tidewater Regional Police Academy in Hampton Virginia to complete the state requirement for certification. In the academy, I was always clowning around playing jokes on the other cadets and just being an idiot. Is there a pattern here?

One training day we had the American Red Cross present a class on CPR and Basic First Aid. The female instructor brought a life size manikin type doll she called Annie, to teach us the proper way of doing CPR.

At break time, I told a cadet friend of mine, Patrick (not his real name) from Newport News PD to hang back with me in the class room. We waited for the instructor and the rest of the class to leave the classroom and I told Patrick to watch the door and let me know when the rest of the class was returning back to the classroom.

I took the Annie doll off the table and I laid her/it on the floor. I unbuckled my belt, uniform pants and dropped them right below my butt. Patrick, who had been watching out the classroom door as instructed, announced that our classmates were on their way in. With my pants down, I laid on top of Annie. Now readers, don't get ahead of me. I was expecting my classmates to enter first and see me. I intended for them to have a good laugh and get back to the training. Well dear readers that did not happen. The Red Cross lady and her supervisor, who just happened to pay us a visit, walked in the classroom first.

Talk about a huge embarrassment for all parties involved. The ladies from the Red Cross both made an about face and went straight to the academy directors office. As I was putting myself back together, Patrick was actually on the floor laughing.

I was later summoned to the director's office and threatened with being kicked out of the academy, the university and the state. He even threatened to have my birthday taken away and turn me into a frog.

Anyway dear readers. I must of have had ADD, because I continued with a few other events.

•

It just so happened that the following idiotic event was a few weeks later. Again, we had an instructor, lady type, who was going to teach us how to handle people that are blind, site deficient or whatever the political correct BS term is. Anyway, this lady instructor was instructing on the proper way of guiding a blind person when walking with them. She provided the class with eye mask that are made to place over your eyes and you cannot see anything.

She paired up in twos and had one of us to cover our eyes with the eye masks and the other cadet guide us down the hallway. She had the entire class participating. Well, it just so happen, Patrick was my partner for this exercise and I was the one to cover my eyes and be led around.

I don't know what I was thinking at the time, I thought I would have some fun so I asked Patrick to make sure he bumps me into one particular female cadet and I will grab her breast as if by mistake. Everyone including the female cadets was having fun during this exercise, being led and bumping into walls. Patrick agreed and so I placed the mask over my eyes. We walked out into the hallway where I could hear laughter and people bumping into walls and trash cans.

Patrick led me to what I thought was the cadet I asked him for and so gently I reached out with the back of my hands and rubbed someone's breast, except it wasn't the female cadet's breast. It was the lady instructor who happened to cross our path. I heard a shout that didn't sound too friendly and I pulled off my mask. It was this instructor standing in front of me with her mouth wide open. I began apologizing profusely and Patrick again was laughing. This poor instructor didn't know what to do. She finally gathered her composure and apologized to me for being in the way. I thought for sure I would again be called into the director's office. As far as Patrick, I never again asked him partake in any of my schemes.

●

Prior to graduating the academy, I did commit a couple of more schemes without the assistance of my friend Patrick. One was during water survival training in a large swimming pool. Being a certified diver and Marine, spawn of Poseidon (I said you may see this again) one can only guess what I did. I'll leave it at that. It caused me to be made to sit at the edge of the pool while everyone else completed their exercise.

I will say that the Academy, including the staff had their revenge on me during graduation ceremony.

During the graduation ceremony of the Tide Water Regional Police Academy of which several classes were graduating that day, the entire auditorium was full of visitors including officials representing different cities of eastern Virginia. When it was our class's turn to receive our diplomas, for some reason my name was called at the very last. After my name was called, I walked up to the director, who was handing out diplomas. He handed me a rolled up official looking paper like the other cadets had gotten. After receiving it in my hand he asked me in front of all watching to unroll it and read it. I unrolled the diploma and saw that it was blank. I guess my facial expression must have given me away because I saw the entire audience laughing. They were in on the joke or pay back done to me. I did receive the real diploma shortly after.

I guess I had that coming.

•

After graduation I returned to Hampton University Police Department. Hampton University is located right next to the James River across the bay from the Norfolk Naval Base. The University itself was an old plantation founded in 1868 as a school to provide education to freemen or former slaves. In 1878 it developed a program to teach Native Americans. On the campus are several old buildings still in use today. One such building is Phoenix Hall. The three story building at one time was an old high school with plenty of stories behind it. One such story as told to me by police officers working there was that it was haunted. I used that bit of information to my advantage for my still present practical jokes.

On the night shift, I was assigned a partner, a young black police officer, Sean (not real name) who admittedly believed in the haunted stories of Phoenix Hall. As part of our duties, we had to check all campus buildings making sure lights were out and doors locked. One evening I got with the shift sergeant and told him I wanted to play a trick on Sean and the Sergeant agreed. I went up the third floor of Phoenix Hall and turned a light on in one of the rooms. While I remained upstairs, the shift supervisor called Sean on the radio and directed him to Phoenix Hall to check the third floor because a light was left on. I could hear Sean on my portable radio when he reluctantly agreed.

I waited upstairs and the sergeant went to the front of the building. Sean arrived at the rear of the building and entered thru the rear entrance. I could hear him slowly and I mean slowly coming up the stairs. As he reached the third floor I started banging on the wall lockers. I was damn lucky I did not get shot, because Sean was having trouble drawing his weapon and running at the same time. When he reached the rear exit door the rest of the shift were parked with their headlights on facing the exit door. Sean was not too happy with me after that.

•

Hampton University is the home of an old cemetery that dates back to the Civil War. Stories by old timers were that of a headless man, supposedly a slave, has been seen in the area. One rainy night, I was assigned to partner up with Sean to patrol the campus. Since it was raining, I was wearing my rain coat and sitting on the passenger seat. As we patrolled by the cemetery, knowing Sean was always afraid of talking about it, I ask him to tell me the story about the headless man that has been seen in the area.

Sean began the story as I quietly sat in the passenger seat on that rainy night. As Sean was talking, I slowly pulled up the raincoat over my head as he talked. I button the top buttons of the rain coat where the collar was just over my head. As if on que, Sean turned to look at me when a flash of lightning struck. Sean looked and all that he sees is a headless person with a yellow rain coat sitting next to him. It is hard to describe the look of horror that he had. I had to bail out of the car, I was laughing so hard. Sean did not like being my partner after that.

•

On the night shift at HUPD, at times we would meet with officers from the Hampton Police Department for breakfast in the city. One early morning my partner and I met with two HPD patrol officers at a 24 hours restaurant for early breakfast. It was about 0400 hours (4 o'clock in the am). We sat at a booth next to a large window. While having breakfast, we heard loud rumbling as motorcycles were arriving to this restaurant. At the time my older brother Joe was about to retire from the US Army and had been stationed up the road at Fort Eustis, Virginia. Joe had always been a motorcycle rider and presently was affiliated with a local outlaw motorcycle gang (OMG). Although he was not a patched member, he often rode with them and in many ways acted like them. Anyway we were having breakfast and my partner sitting across the table from me said *"Hey, we are being mooned, somebody is mooning us"*. I looked over and see this naked ass plastered on the window from the outside. I told them not to worry, it's only my brother. The bikers walked in laughing. One of them stopped at our table and told me "hey officer, your brother is crazy".

My brother Joe, although still on active duty in the US Army, had a part time job as a DJ at the local topless/biker bar outside the base. He was close to retirement, having done 2 tours in Vietnam and had that "I could care less" attitude. As I mentioned before, he was not a patched member but rode with an OMG and was well known among them. One evening he asked me to join him at the bar he worked at. We sat at a table having a cold one when OMG members began to walk in. I immediately recognized one of them that I had arrested for public intoxication weeks before. I whispered to Joe about the arrest and nodded towards the bike gang member. Joe, shouts out to the individuals telling them, *"Hey Renegade Jim, come here, my brother arrested you"*. I didn't know whether to prepare for knock down drag down fight, or get the hell out. The OMG members walked to our table and I began to brace myself for trouble. The president of the club places his big hand on my shoulder and pointed to 'Renegade Jim' and asked "Did you arrest him"? I told him I did and he began patting me on my back saying good job. They all had a good laugh and bought us rounds of drinks. The president of the bike gang invited me to a party but I politely declined the invitation.

Hidalgo Police Department

I left Virginia and moved back to Texas. I wound up in the border town of Hidalgo Texas. Hidalgo is nestled between the much larger city of McAllen and the Rio Grande River. Opposite the river, on the Mexican side lies Reynosa a large populated city in the Mexican state of Tamaulipas. I got hired in Hidalgo as a police officer. At that time the department had approximately 10 police officers including the Chief of Police. The city itself was mostly quiet and peaceful except for the heavy traffic crossing the border.

•

El Diablo

One slow Sunday morning, I was supervising the day shift. At that time the department had grown to about 18 patrol officers. Traffic was very slow and the day started out as being boring. At the morning briefing I challenged the patrol officers on who could make the most arrest. We were a total of 4 patrol officers on the day shift. After briefing, everyone headed to their patrol cars and after checking the vehicle went out to find bad guys. One of the officers, on the shift, told me he would beat me in making arrests. Well, that sounds like a personal challenge. Like I mentioned, it was Sunday and an unusual slow day. I could hear on the police radio the patrol officers were making traffic stops and trying to find DWI drivers or wanted persons.

We later received a call from dispatch of a theft that had just occurred at a shoe store near the International Bridge.

At that time, there was a semi homeless man everyone called El Diablo. El Diablo had a habit of being arrested almost every week for various reasons like public intoxication to shop lifting. When Carr and I arrived at the shoe store on the theft call, the first person I see standing outside the shoe store was 'El Diablo'. I noticed something different about him. El Diablo was wearing a nice clean ironed white shirt and he was clean shaven. He saw me, immediately walked up to the shoe store and the first thing he started telling me was, he was sober and going to church. I really didn't pay much attention to what he was trying to tell me and continued into the store.

Once inside the store Carr and I met with the store manager who told us the suspect left the store with a pair of shoes and had made it across the bridge into Mexico. Carr and I were both disappointed because that would have been an arrest. I then remember El Diablo standing outside the store and thought, he is always good for an arrest since he was always drunk no matter the time of day. I ran outside and El Diablo was still standing outside. When he saw the look on my face, he knew something bad was about to happen to him. He began telling me he didn't do anything and he was sober and was waiting for a ride to church.

My mind was in the arrest mode so I placed handcuffs on him. He started crying and telling me in Spanish "please officer Garica, I am not drunk and I'm waiting for my ride to church". I wouldn't have it, someone was going to jail that day and El Diablo was always a good arrest. The other officer at the scene told me, "Sarge, what are you doing? He is not drunk". I gave a wink to the officer and placed the upset El Diablo in the back seat of my patrol car. I drove a couple of blocks, pulled over and released El Diablo. He assured me he was a changed man. I never did see him after that. No arrest were made that Sunday which was unusual.

•

Working in a border town, we always had problems with illegal border crossers and especially border bandits. We had a problem with one certain border bandit who would help unsuspecting groups of people wanting to get into the US, to illegally get across the river and upon reaching the US side of the border this bandido would rob these poor people and/ or sometimes sexually assault the women. He then would swim back across the border into Mexico. At that time our police chief instructed me and another officer with a military background as well to change into camouflage clothing and work the river side to apprehend this bandido. Our instructions was to catch this bandit without fail. The officer, who I will call Mike and I would work the brush area at a favorite crossing for this particular bandit. After a couple of days, the media contacted the police chief to ascertain what was being done about these bandits. The chief invited the media to join our operation. We reluctantly took two news people with us on one operation. I purposely guided them through rough terrain, under and over obstacles. They didn't last very long.

A day later, Mike and I decided to get to the river before day break and get set up. We entered the brush area and picked out a good hide spot and waited. Incidentally the area around the river was home to other critters besides human traffic. I have come in contact with coral snakes, black widows, scorpions, large nest of yellow jacket wasp and other creepy crawlies that would make one think twice about volunteering going into this type of terrain. This didn't bother me as much after being in the jungles of the Philippines or the Mojave Desert. Anyway our faces were painted up with camo paint and we got set up in a good spot to catch this bandit. I told Mike to remain where he was and I snaked my way around towards the east, heading down river. I was moving at a snail's pace when I noticed some movement under some brush. I got on my stomach and began crawling towards the movement. After what it seemed a very long slow crawl I saw our suspect sitting under a large bush watching the river. Mike and I were wearing ear mics so our radio traffic could not be heard by anyone else. I whispered in my radio mic to my partner Mike, *"I have eyes on the suspect"* and told him to come towards me along the river's edge in case the suspect decides to go that way. I carefully moved my way towards the suspect, trying hard not to make any noise while stepping and low crawling through the thick brush.

I finally made it to just behind the suspect and waited for my partner Mike. As soon as I heard Mike's moving my way in the brush, the suspect heard it as well. With my Beretta 9mm in my right hand, I eased up to the suspect and placed my left hand on his shoulder.

The suspect slowly turned his head and sees this green and black face wearing a boonie hat, staring back at him with a gun pointed to his head. His eyes opened wide and it appeared he wanted to scream but for some reason could not. I felt the muscles on his shoulders tense up as if he wanted to run towards the river. By that time Mike was already in front of him and we caught our suspect.

I will say, eventually the bandido had to be released because none of his victims could be found or wanted to testify. A Korean family that had fell victim to this suspect could not be found. After a few days in the county jail. The suspect was deported back to Mexico.

•

A few years later, while I was commander of our Border Crisis Intervention Team, I was patrolling the river and saw that very same suspect mentioned above lying under a tree next to the river. I walked up to him and immediately recognized him. The bandido was laying on his side and since he was not wearing a shirt I notice what looked like some kind of wound possibly a gunshot wound on his back. There was blood and tiny bubbles coming from the apparent wound. I recognized he was possibly shot through the lung. He was having problems breathing. I contacted our dispatch and ask for an ambulance and Border Patrol (BP) for assistance. At that time, I did not have any first aid kit but I tried to make him as comfortable as possible until the ambulance arrived.

The suspect was barely talking and I asked him what happened. He said he was shot on the Mexican side of the river by the Mexican police. He had swam across with a hole in his lung. I notice he was turning a greyish color. The ambulance and BP arrived. Later that day I was informed the suspect was dead on arrival.

•

As a patrol officer, I tried to bring some happiness to even the arrestees. One example, I printed a sign to hang on the back of the cage divider of my patrol vehicle. Anyone arrested and placed in the rear seat could read the sign. The sign read, *'My pet Tarantula escaped from her cage somewhere in this vehicle. If you see her, please remain calm and let me know'.* You would be surprised how many calm, handcuffed prisoners I transported.

At the Hidalgo Police Department we had the responsibility to patrol the international bridge and respond to any incidents on or around the bridge. Early in my career at HPD, the bridge board hired private security to patrol the bridge to keep pedestrians moving and street venders away from the cars. One day while on patrol, we received a call about a person drowning in the Rio Grande near the bridge. Apparently, a female security was patrolling on top of the bridge and observed a human body floating in the river. She reported it as a drowning subject to our dispatcher. I understood from dispatch, a person was having trouble swimming and was possibly drowning. I responded and was the first on scene. The security met me under the bridge and pointed up stream to what appeared like a male subject floating towards us with the current.

At this point, I am thinking this person was recently seen swimming and began to drown. I removed my duty belt, ballistic vest and dove in the water. Again a Marine thing here remember? Son of Poseidon. Anyway I'm swimming against the current to the floating body. When I reached the body, I am still thinking CPR, saving a life. I grabbed him from the hair and the entire scalp came off my hand. Dear gentile readers, I started thinking otherwise by now, saying a few choice words to the God of the sea, dispatch and the security who called this in. This guy had been dead for a while. I let the scalp go and began swimming away from the "floater". By that time several Customs and Border Patrol agents along with my supervisor were on the bank and told me to go ahead and bring him in to the edge. I figured what the hell, I'm in the water with this body, grabbed it by the shirt and brought it in. When we pulled it out of the water and turned it around, the nose, eyes and the flesh of his fingers were missing. Fish, turtle or alligator gar had apparently feasted on this person.

I was still angry with myself for trying to be the hero. I grabbed my gear from the security officer who was in the process of vomiting. I took the rest of the day off and probably showered for 2 hours.

●

As law enforcement instructor, myself and another sergeant were sent to an OC pepper spray instructor's course so we could return and train our officers in the use of this non-lethal use of force. The OC pepper spray is about 95 percent capsicum which is the main ingredient of hot chili pepper.

The class was held in San Antonio and instructed by a captain from the South Carolina highway patrol, Captain James Braddock (not real name). The captain was contracted by the pepper spray company to train police instructors on the use of the product.

At the beginning of the class, the captain asked for any volunteers to get sprayed at the end of the course. I was sitting towards the front of the classroom and raised my hand.

The captain asked if I happened to be a Marine. When I told him I was, he said *"I knew it, I knew it, every time, I ask for volunteers, some dumb ass Marine raises his hands first"*. He knew us well. As promised, I was the first to get pepper sprayed during class. Two of my class mates stood at each side of me to hold me up in case I went to the ground while being sprayed. I didn't go to the ground, but as soon as the spray hit my face, my eyes involuntary shut and my face began burning. I had to immediately wash my face.

Incidentally, my younger brother Charlie was completing his probationary police training at our department and he sprayed a subject in our book-in room when the subject started fighting with the arresting officer. The remnants of the spray was caught up in the jail's air condition ducts and spread throughout the building. Thank you Charlie.

Border Crises Intervention Team

As a Sergeant with the Hidalgo Police Department, I had other duties that I actually volunteered for. I was the department's Training Coordinator, Firearms Instructor and even the Field Training Coordinator.

The Chief of Police at that time again knew of the problems we were having with border bandits. I was instructed to help curtail this problem. I did some homework and came up with the concept of a team of local and federal officers that could respond to criminal situations within our Area of Responsibility (AOR) along the border.

I drafted a Needs Assessment and Mission Statement and went before our Chief of Police with this concept. The Chief gave me the green light to go forward but I would have to come up with the logistics through a different source because of our department's budget. I told him I had that covered as well. This team was designated as the Border Crisis Intervention Team (BCIT).

Being that we bordered an International Border and it would require the assistance of federal agencies, I sent copies of the Needs Assessment and Mission Statement to two sitting US senators that happened to be from

Texas. In the letter, I asked for their direction on how to proceed with this plan and the possibility of obtaining aid from government sources. I received responses from both senators office informing me they have forwarded the plan to the Department of Justice (DOJ) and I should be hearing from them.

Shortly after, I received letters from the DOJ to set up a meeting with the Border Patrol and they would like to assist anyway they can. I met with supervisors of the Border Patrol and US Customs. They agreed to provide us with equipment and personnel whenever possible. I later met with the chiefs of police with some of the surrounding cities including the county sheriff. I showed them my Mission Statements and Needs Assessments and was laughed out of their office. I was told by a certain sheriff (do the math) that we did not have a big problem on the border. Years later, as I write this, I see the problems they are having now on the border. That "certain sheriff" is now sitting in a federal prison for other reasons.

The BCIT went on as plan, thanks to our Chief of Police at the time. US Customs, pre 9/11 was still under the jurisdiction of the Department of the Treasury, provided us with all the ammunition we wanted. They even assisted us in building up our gun range. On several occasion, during our firearms training, I would have the team run over the levies carrying a small log. They called it a telephone pole (technicalities). After getting over the levy, the team would drop the ittie bittie log, draw their weapon and fire at 3x5 cards. Lord help them if they missed. 'Num-nuts', if you read this, I bet you still have fond memories.

The local US Marine recruiters got involved as well. They provided the Physical Training (PT) portion of the training. Again, Num-nuts do you recall? For some reason, during our running exercise along the river, I kept hearing "I hate you Sarge". These men loved me.

•

The team participated in a number of border operations. Spending many long hours in the brush, during the night, along the river with night vision devices provided by the border patrol. Some operations had positive results.

The BCIT was coming along pretty well until I deployed to Kosovo and the team was disbanded.

We did some training with Border Patrol Tactical (Bor-Tac) units and after I had deployed to Kosovo, I met up with some of these same Bor-Tac members in Kosovo when they were deployed to Albania under the Department of Justice to help train our Albanian counterparts.

•

Since being a member of the Border Crisis Intervention Team required everyone being in the best shape possible and I as commander of the team, I had to make sure I was in just as good of shape. During our runs along the river, I always believed a leader leads from the front so I ran up in front of the team. That is what LEADer means to me. There is a difference between a leader and a supervisor or manager. Every opportunity I would run trails alongside the Rio Grande river. Sometimes my oldest daughter Jackie who was on the cross country team in High School would join me on my runs. She didn't run in combat boots though.

•

A Cowboy's Word

While working at the Hidalgo Police Department, I lived at the El Texano Ranch. The ranch was once owned by an old ranching family and it use to be a working cattle ranch before much of the land was sold or donated to the City of Hidalgo and school district. When I first moved to Hidalgo, the ranch was near its end of existence but still had some cattle on the property. Behind the ranch office stood a barn with horse stalls adjacent to it. The barn had a second floor with a bedroom built on its second floor. I lived at the ranch for very little rent as I helped take care of the cattle. On the ground floor was the kitchen and bath that included a large barn area. It was the perfect place for a single cowboy/police officer. I later was joined by my good friend "Chon" (the Americanos pronounced it Sean) who was a true cowboy and worked for the US Department of Agriculture (USDA) as a Tick Rider. Tick riders are modern day cowboys hired by the USDA to ride assigned trails along the Rio Grande to locate any stray livestock that happened to cross the river from Mexico. The USDA had set a 700 mile long quarantine line between Brownsville and Del Rio Texas. Each tick rider is assigned certain sections to ride and locate signs of any type of livestock that had crossed and may be infested with the fever tick. Many of these cattle were known to infest US livestock with various types of disease thus causing entire ranches to be quarantined. Chon's area of patrol was just south of the ranch I lived on so he moved a camper trailer next to the barn on the ranch. Often, I would get invited to ride alongside Chon learning the trade. Chon taught me a lot about cowboying since his family has been ranching in south Texas since the late 1800's. Many times when he was off or on vacation, I was allowed to ride the trails along the river. Whenever stray cattle were found out in the brush country they were roped and held. Other tick riders would arrive with portable pens. The livestock would be transported to an assigned quarantine area to be held for final disposition.

Occasionally tick riders would get day jobs or part time work in moving cattle on different ranches and I would tag-along with my horse Cochise.

One weekend, I was looking forward to going to the PRCA Rodeo in Los Fresnos Texas. I had planned on going that Saturday. Being excited about the rodeo, I had already forgotten, my promised to Chon I would help him and the other tick rider's move and load cattle at the Doffin Ranch. On the Friday evening, I went to a nightclub that had live music with the intentions of dancing and having a good time as cowboys do. I went to the club and met two young ladies from Colorado who were going to barrel race at the rodeo. Later that evening, they mentioned they wanted to go to Mexico. Of course my dumb butt volunteered to take them. I must have been feeling real good, because, I have never driven in Reynosa Mexico let alone go by myself. So we left the club, hopped into my truck and drove into Mexico. We visited a few clubs and one of the girls mentioned about going to "Boys Town". For you gentile readers, that's where those "painted ladies" sell their wares. Now, like I mentioned earlier, I've never driven in Mexico much less been to Boys Town. I volunteered to take them. We were having a good time. I had to stop in almost every corner and ask people standing around "*Donde esta la casas de las Putas*". They would point to the direction and off we go. We finally made it to "*La Zona Roja*" and were met by a guard at the main entrance. The girls had to be signed in, I guess to not be confused when we would exit the place. Within the compound there were several individual bars in a plaza type area. With a big smile and two Colorado cowgirls in each arm we visited the bars.

I guess it was not surprising that none of these painted ladies asked me if I needed servicing since I had two girls with me (I will keep it clean readers). Anyway the evening or early morning wore on. When we finally walked out the sun was up, the birds were chirping loudly. Yes, it was early morning. We made our way back across the border. I recall thinking; I must be the luckiest feller in Texas. I have these two cowgirls who agreed to sleep it off at the ranch. As we entered the ranch property, I rounded the corner of the ranch office and see Chon standing next to his pick-up truck hitched to the horse trailer. Both his and my horse were saddled and loaded. Chon watched as I drove up and saw me with these two buckle bunnies in my truck. He approached us and said "*partner, you promised me you would help gather cows today and I have everything ready to go*". It suddenly occurred to me I had given my word I would help. I know, I was probably looking ragged since I had been out all night and probably drunk myself sober if that is possible. I reluctantly agreed and escorted the two girls upstairs to my room. As they were getting ready for bed, I was putting my boots and spurs on. Chon was down stairs honking the horn to make sure I didn't forget. Anyway, I went downstairs, the girls got into my bed. Did I mention this was the summer, in Deep South Texas and it was hot?

The cattle were deep in the brush or under large mesquite trees. The mesquite in south Texas grew large with limbs that spread out. On hot days livestock would gather underneath for shade. Cochise, my horse, worked out to be a good cow pony because he did all the work. I was in no shape to be out there. We later broke for lunch. Lunch was brought out to us by the rancher's wife. Feeling a bit under the weather, I did not feel like eating so I lay in the horse trailer nursing a bad headache. I guess the ranch owner was told about my situation because he walked over to where I was laying and handed me two aspirins. He said "here son, I hear you need this". I could hear the other cowboys laughing.

When break was over, we finished loading the last of the cattle. Late that evening we headed back to the ranch where we lived. At the ranch, we unloaded the horses, washed them down and fed. I went upstairs to my room and both girls were already up and dressed. They needed to be dropped off to gather their horses and head to Los Fresnos. I was invited but turned down the invite. I went back to the ranch and died.

So there you go readers, A Cowboy's word

•

Cochise

My horse Cochise turned out to be a little scoundrel. Chon and I would at times host Bar-B-Ques at the ranch for other tick riders and visitors. We would be hanging outside enjoying the evening with our friends; I would leave Cochise loose around the barn area to eat the grass (I didn't have a lawn mower). We were drinking beer out of bottles and some would leave their beer bottles laying around, Cochise would sneak up from behind grab a bottle with his mouth and turn it up to drink what was inside. At the time we didn't know this. Someone would accuse someone else of drinking his beer until we caught Cochise with a bottle in his mouth. Cochise was never invited to our parties again.

•

Prior to my departure of the Hidalgo Police Department so seek new adventures, we were at a stage where we needed and hired more police officers. I began the first Field Training Officer's program. Thanks to the Houston Police Department whose field training program we modeled after. I got the Texas Commission of Law Enforcement Officer Standard and Education (TCLOSE) to certify our department as a training center, frequently hosting training for our department and other departments. I initiated the first Officer Friendly program in our school district. I like to think I left HPD in a better position than I found it.

CHAPTER III

International Police Officer (IPO)

Kosovo

I am not going to get into the politics regarding Kosovo and its current status. That is not what this book is about. However, with NATO forces and the United Nations, I will say the United States, under the sitting president got involved and thus we were sent there as an International Police force, training and monitor mission,

In August of 1999, while I was a police officer with the Hidalgo Police Department. I answered an ad from the US Department of State (DOS) calling for police officers with at least 8 years' experience, to go to Kosovo and help train a new established Kosovo Police Force (KPS).

The United Nations Security Council had just implemented UN Resolution 1244 which gave powers to the United Nations Mission In Kosovo (UNMIK) to oversee a newly establish government.

Kosovo had been on a long political and territorial dispute between Serbia and ethnic Albanians.

The US Department of State issued the contract to supply police officers to a large logistics company. I applied and was soon hired. We were first sent to the American Airline training center at DFW airport for further exams and training. At that time approximately 200 police officers from around the US answered the call and arrived at DFW.

While at the training center we were given further physical and mental exam along with classes by the US DOS on international rule of law and customs.

After approximately 10 days we were deployed to Kosovo on a UN contracted former Russian air force cargo plane. That in itself was an experience. During the flight, the Russian pilots allowed us to enter the cockpit and sit in the navigator seat. Kuhl huh?

Upon arrival to Prisitina airport in Kosovo, we were met by armed Russian soldiers. We hadn't been issued any weapons at that point. After we exited the plane we boarded busses that were near the runway. As we neared the almost demolished terminal, the Russian soldiers didn't appear to be welcoming us to Pristina. I noticed several of them were still in bandages and appeared to scowl as we disembarked at the airport terminal.

The terminal itself was something to be considered. Most of the glass on windows surrounding the terminal was blown out. What appeared to be the remnants of a rocket was sticking out from the top of the terminal. We noticed many of the surrounding villages were still smoking or on fire after bombing runs from NATO forces.

From what I understand, Russia was not part of the NATO deployment as they sided with Serbia. However they raced to Prisitina airport to take control of the airport during the bombing of Pristina. Russia had wanted to receive a sector of Kosovo independent of NATO but it was refused by NATO.

During this time a British pop singer, I won't mention any name here that was famous for his song 'Your Beautiful" (do the math) was a Captain of a British armored brigade. The Captain was ordered to stop the Russian from taking the airport in Pristina. The captain hesitated citing he would rather face a court martial then the Russians or start World War III. The Russian forces were preparing with reinforcements to keep the airport.

My first year in Kosovo (Aug 1999 – Sept 2000) I was assigned to the United nations Mission in Kosovo (UNMIK) Border Police, stationed at the General Yankovic Border. Our duties were to check all persons entering Kosovo, checking documents and vehicles. Many of the returning refugees did not have documents upon their return to Kosovo so it was left up to us to vet them. Not knowing the language at the time (Serbian or Albanian) we were assigned Language Assistance or translators that were fluent in both languages and English.

On our team (team 2) we were police officers from the United States, Germany, Philippines, India, Pakistan, Russia and Ukraine. Every one of the officers except the US were national police in their respective countries. The US officers, we were police contractors. We all got along pretty well. Some of the Russian border officers we worked with were former KGB officers or agents. We had a pretty good team. Our duty times were 12 hour shifts, 7 days a week. Those of us that had to travel from Pristina to the border had to start our trip earlier because at times it took us 4 to 6 hours to make the trip. UNMIK had provided us with Toyota 4-Runners that were painted red and white. It looked like a Coca Cola can, so it was called a Coca Cola vehicle. At that time, four to five UNMIK officers were assigned to a single vehicle. It was the driver's duty to make the rounds and pick us up and drop us off after our shifts every day.

The Kosovo mission was divided into five regions by the UN and NATO (KFOR-Kosovo Force). The United States had the southeastern region, Germany had the southwestern region, France had the northern region. The British had the Pristina region and Italy or Spain had the western region of Kosovo. Within those regions other NATO members were assigned, for instance within the US region, Polish, Ukraine and Arab military troops were assigned to patrol the region.

On our border, Polish KFOR troops were assigned to secure our border station and after their rotation, Greek KFOR took over the duties. The drive to and from work was always quite an adventure. The major highways was always congested with military convoys. Roads were in bad need of repair and some of the other roads were yet not cleared of land mines.

Each shift was assigned translators or Language Assistants (LA.s). I made it a point to learn Albanian as the majority of the travelers were ethnic Albanian. I would ask the LA's to teach me phrases and I would write them down and practice every day. One of the first I asked to learn was "welcome to Kosovo". An LA we called Wilson thought me 'Mirecerdit nge Kosovas' or mirepritur shtepi'. As refugee buses arrived, I would board the bus and welcome them back to their home. These passengers who on their last time in Kosovo were forced to leave, see an American board the bus and welcome them back in their own language. I had many of the old Albanian passengers get up hug, kiss me on both cheeks and cry. I really felt bad for these people.

•

While on the day shift one day, the border crossing had these little kiosk between the lanes with doors. It was very cold and there were a lot of birds around eating pieces of bread everyone one was dropping. I got a piece of bread and sprinkled crumbs around the kiosk and inside the kiosk. I had left the door partially opened so the birds would follow the bread crumbs in. I waited until there were about 12 to 15 birds in the Kiosk and I slammed the door shut, trapping the birds inside. I quickly got into the Kiosk with the birds, closing the door behind me. That day I was wearing a heavy duty jacket. One by one I began catching the birds and stuffing them in my jacket. After I collected all the birds. I waited for the next refugee bus to arrive. When the next bus drove up I stood in front of the bus with a stern face as if to not let it go any further.

I waited until everyone in the bus had their eyes on me as I am sure they did not know what was going on. I am sure many believed they were going to be turned back. I unzipped my jacket and all they see is a bunch of birds flying out of my jackets. The passengers in the bus began cheering and laughing.

Many of these people left the country in a bad way. They were forced out by the Serbians. Many escaped extermination by leaving their belonging behind and going over the mountains with only the clothes on their backs. Like I mentioned before, I will not get into the political aspects of Kosovo but the stories of the atrocities done to the Kosovar Albanians, left an impression on me. So anything I could do to bring a smile to their faces upon their return to their homeland I gladly did.

•

One day while working the Jankovic border, I was assigned to the primary inspection checkpoint and one of my American colleague, was working the secondary inspection. I was busy checking the passengers on a bus, when I heard the officer raise his voice. Being an American police officer, trained to respond to come to the aid of any officer, I went to help my colleague. When I arrived, I saw him struggling with a male subject. I immediately jumped on the subject's back so that my momentum could take him to the ground. This subject remained on his feet and the officer and I were trying to bring him down to the ground. He was powerful and did not want to go down. At that time the two Philippine officers working the checkpoint came to our aid. Renato Sun and Wilson Villanueva (not real names) jumped in to assist us in bringing this suspect down. At some point I was still on the suspect's back when Renato jumped on my back. By this time the suspect was swinging his arms and resisting. With all our weight on the person, I heard a loud snap and saw the subject's leg bend to one side in an odd angle. I immediately think that we broke this guy's leg and my brain goes into over drive, thinking about me losing my job, being sent back to the states.

I'm trying to get my weight off the suspect, Renato and Wilson are on my back still trying to get him down. I then see Renato kicking the suspect's broken leg and I am about to go into cardiac arrest wondering "why is he kicking this guy's leg". It turns out the leg was a prosthetic that had snapped. The suspect was hopping on one leg saying "no problem, no problem". The American colleague and I were so relieved that it was not a real leg that broke and we let this poor subject return (hop) back to Macedonia. It is where we wanted him to go in the first place.

●

The General Yankovic border crossing point is located on the Kosovo and Macedonia border. During a time while working the Yankovic border, the Polish KFOR rotated out, the Greek military took over the border security duties. The Greek military were fun to work with as well. However we were reminded by the Greeks that the Macedonians as they called themselves were not true Macedonian. The country of Macedonia was formerly known as the Former Yugoslav Republic of Macedonia (FYROM). The majority of the inhabitants are primarily ethnic Slavs. A large number of ethnic Albanians live in Macedonia.

•

On my first trip home during the Christmas holidays of 1999, I was flying out of the airport in Skopia, Macedonia. The airport was still in turmoil with all the governmental organizations, non-governmental organization, refugees, news media and NATO troops trying to catch a flight out. It was first come first serve seating. For us westerners it was rather chaotic. No type of a queue was formed. I was sitting in the airport lobby waiting for my flight number to be announced. Every time a flight would be called for passengers to board, a hoard of passenger's, mainly locals, would rush up and try to be the first in the queue. I recall thinking these people had no concept of waiting in line. As I sat there, I began talking to a Navy SEAL sitting next to me, he was flying to the states for the holidays as well. This SEAL had been in-country before and during the war. As our plane arrived, the announcement came over the intercom that passengers with a diplomatic or official passport could board the flight first. At that moment almost everyone in the terminal rushed the boarding ramp. The airport staff were over whelmed. The SEAL pulled a black US Diplomatic passport out of his backpack held it up and at the same time, grabbed the back handle of my military style backpack I had on my back and drug me to the front of the line, telling the lady at the gate "he's with me". Thanks to this SEAL I got to board the flight.

•

During the Balkan war of 1990s, the capital of Macedonia, Skopia was divided with ethnic Albanians on one side of the Vadar River and ethnic Slav Macedonian on the other.

In 2001 a conflict occurred between the Macedonia government and the ethnic Albanians living in the north and western part of Macedonia. The war ended when NATO troops intervened and a ceasefire was agreed under the Orhid Agreement. During this conflict, my then wife and my friend and fellow UNMIK police officer, whom I will call Joe; wife was flying into Skopia Macedonia. The plan was for Joe and me to drive to Macedonia and pick up our wives and drive them to Kosovo for a visit. The fighting began between the Macedonian military and the ethnic

Albanians. Joe and I were worried about getting across the border in time to pick up our wives and getting back. The border crossing points were constantly closing at the whim of the Macedonian government or the troops on our side of the border. Joe and I were in a white UN Toyota 4 Runner with UN markings on the doors. We got to the border and found it was closed to all traffic except for military traffic. KFOR had their own route around the crossing point, so Joe and I went that route. We were not stopped by anyone.

We made it to the Skopia airport and picked up our passengers (wives). On the way back to Kosovo, the Macedonian military resumed its bombing on an ethnic Albanian village on the side of a mountain. We could see the village being hit by bombs. I remember my wife asking what is that over there pointing to some burning structures on the side of a hill. I saw several building burning and the area exploding with debris and smoke. I told her that the villagers were just burning trash because they had no way of getting rid of the garbage so they blow it up. I never told her what was really happening until much later.

●

The first days, even months in Kosovo, everything was still in a mess. The UN and NATO were trying to get situated. There was no power, no drinking water unless purchased out in the streets. Telephone service was almost non-existent. Everyone one of us in country were trying to get word home that we arrived and were safe. After a few days we got word that a local bar had a SAT (satellite) phone and would let us use it to make a call home. We found the Kukri bar that was owned by a British gentleman we come to know as "John". We went to John and asked if he had a phone that we can use to call our families. John told us he had satellite phone and we were welcome to use but he would have to charge us what he was charge for its use. The three of us made quick phone calls just long enough to tell our families we had arrived and were safe. Thank you John. I will not speculate why John was in the country and owned a bar. The Kukri bar was an oasis for almost every international police or civilian personnel. The food was good and the beer even better. Many thanks John. Cheers.

Victor's Ski Trip

As mentioned before, although we worked on the General Yankovic border, most of us lived in Pristina some 60 miles to the north. We lived in a 2 floor home (flat) with the owners, a doctor and his wife living on the ground floor and my roommate Victor and I on the second floor. That first winter was harsh and the roadways and trails were always icy. The flat we lived in was located on a semi steep hill.

One cold evening Victor and I decided to walk to the center of the city to have dinner. Victor had just received a pair of combat boots from his mother in Virginia. These boots looked like the old military jump boots that laced up. I waited for Victor to put the boots on and lace them up. The night air was brutally cold and all the streets were iced over and eerily quiet. We walked out into the courtyard of the flat and through the large metal gate. I unlocked the gate and allowed Victor to walk through. I stepped into the small street as well and turned around to lock the gate behind me. I soon heard a long scream and I saw Victor sliding down the street carrying a trash barrel. It seemed like he was gaining speed going down the hill. I broke out into a laughter while Victor was trying to maintain his balance still holding on to the barrel. As he reached the bottom of the hill, Victor fell still holding the barrel. I too almost fell because I was laughing so hard. I carefully made my way to Victor's location. He asked if I would go back and get his other boots. He never wore those new boots during the winter.

•

In January of 2000, I was transferred to the Pristina airport to work passport control. At the time, only 4 to 6 civilian flights were arriving and departing from the airport. On most of the flights coming in, were refugees returning to Kosovo. The rest of the flights were military flights.

While working passport control we had a flight come in from the United Kingdom. The passengers came in and I see this tall beautiful woman wearing a large hat. Behind her were several aids carrying her baggage.

This beautiful woman walked up to my booth and handed me her UK Passport. I opened the passport and read that it was issued to Bianca Jaggar (former wife of Mick Jaggar of the Rolling Stones). I had to look two or three times back and forth to the photo and to this lovely woman. She gave me the sweetest smile as I returned her passport not saying anything but smiling at her.

•

Working the airport as border police under the UNMIK Rule of Law, we had the final say so on who can enter Kosovo. A flight had arrived from Slovenia and after checking a few passport, a male subject from the UAE came to my station and handed me two passports. One belonged to him and the other belonged to his wife who was wearing a Hijab covering her entire face. I checked the husband's passport first and allowed him to enter.

The husband stood there and called for his wife wearing the Hajib. I stopped him and told him to keep walking because I had to check his wife passport and view her face. The photo on the wife's passport only had the facial part showing. I told her she had to remove the veil so I can match her face with the photo. Her husband again interrupted me saying I was not allowed to see the face under religious law. I stopped him in mid-sentence and told him that he may continue to pass but she would not pass until I verified the passport photo. I told them both, that is the way it is and if they did not comply, they can turn around and re-board the air plane and go back to where ever they came from. After some grumbling she removed the veil and allowed me see her face.

•

One evening when we got off of our shift at the Pristina Airport, a German Border Police officer and were headed to Pristina, we were stopped by a local Kosovar Albanian that appeared in distress, he ask us for help. The gentleman asked if we can escort him and his family to the hospital because his son had stepped on a land mine. The German colleague driving the marked police van told the driver we help them get to the hospital. With emergency lights and siren we escorted the family to the hospital. After we arrived at the local hospital a woman gets out the rear seat of the vehicle we escorted and she was carrying a young boy. I noticed the lower parts of his legs were gone and I could tell the boy's neck is broken. That memory has always remained with me. Although as a police officer in the states, I have worked accidents with fatalities. I really felt helpless that day and missed my kids even more.

Vrbnica Border

I had returned to Kosovo for my second tour in September of 2000. At that time several of my close friends and Hidalgo PD colleagues had signed up to follow me to Kosovo. Six officers from my old department signed up with the contracting company. Upon our arrival in Kosovo, I first was sent back to General Yankovic border (now known as Hani I Eleizit) then later to the Vrbnica border that shared a border with Albania. That area fell under the Prizren Region HQ.

Prizren is one of the oldest cities of Kosovo and one of the most beautiful cities. I was first assigned as Chief of Operations for the Vrbnica Border Police. Later I was appointed as Deputy Station Commander under a German Bundesgrenzschutz (Border Police) Michael Sterzenbach. Mike originally worked at the Frankfurt airport and got deployed to Kosovo along with a German contingent. As his Deputy Station Commander, it was my duty to oversee the daily operations of the border station and report to the station commander. Michael and I became good friends. We shared plenty of beverages and stories. (Ok, I know what you are thinking by now readers, "he sure enjoys his beverages". Well Yea!) Anyway let me continue here.

One day our border station was schedule for a visit from the head of the Bundesgrenzschutz (Google it), a German General. Michael was all up in arms trying to make sure the border station was ready for the General. I took it in stride because I was confident we were as ready as we could be considering the circumstances and conditions. But for Michael it's a German thing, everything had to be ready and in its proper order. On the day of the arrival of 'his excellency' Michael was extra nervous.

The General arrived by helicopter which landed in the small German military outpost next to our border station. Several UNMIK police staff from Border Police HQ were there as well to greet the General. Everyone except 'moi' were wearing their UN blue beret. I never did like berets much less UN-blue. Michael begged me to wear mine. I promised him I would have it with me. I did have it with me, folded in my back pocket.

Anyway we formerly greeted the general and escorted him to our station. We went up stair to the second floor conference room. The General and his aides sat on one end and Michael and I with some of our staff sat on the other end. I was seated to Michael's right. The General began the meeting by giving a speech on how well this station was doing, blah blah blah. He had heard good things, blah blah. I could sense Michael was nervous as he was about to give his speech to the General.

As I was seated next to Michael the Station Commander, I began rubbing his right leg under the table. I knew the General or his staff could not see. Michael's eyes were about to bulge out of his head. I was trying hard not to laugh out loud and just kept a smile. Michael seemed to get more nervous as I rubbed his leg (yes, only the leg). Michael jumped up and interrupted the General and quickly went into his speech. After the Station Commanders speech the General seemed pretty satisfied and said as much.

After the visitors left Michael turned to me and shouted to be heard over the helicopter's rotor blade noise *"Are you blanking crazy, are you blanking crazy?"*. I just stood there with the biggest grin I could muster. Finally Michael said *"let go get a drink"*. *"Sure boss, lets"* I responded. Now he is making sense.

After Michael returned to Germany, I have maintained contact with him and I have visited with him and his beautiful fiancée at the time. While visiting him at his home outside of Frankfurt Germany, we've sat in his back garden and recalled of old stories and drank good German beer.

•

After Michael's rotation back to Germany, I was appointed Station Commander of the Vrbnica border station. As commander I was allowed to choose my own command staff. As my Deputy Station Commander I chose a member of the German Border Police, as my Chief of Operations an American colleague who I will call Joe. Joe had worked with me at the police department in Hidalgo Texas. I also chose a Bulgarian colleague as Chief of Personnel, an Indian officer as my Chief of Logistics, another German officer as Chief of Investigations. Total we had a staff of approximately 140 international and local border police officers (KPS).

Under UNMIK regulations, most international police officers could not remain in the country for more than 2 years at one time unless special provisions were made between the UN and the host countries or contingent. I was allowed to remain at the Vrbnica BCP for 5 years. In total I was in-country for 8 years. Some of the local staff thought I should become a full citizen and change my name to Bob Gashi.

•

As part of the duties of a Station Commander, I was to scan and asses the Area of Responsibility (AOR) to identify problems and use available resources to develop strategic and tactical plans. I was also responsible for the conduct of all support staff and set mandate for all substations. We were responsible for three additional border substations. My other duties were to liaison with key groups such as military organizations NATO/KFOR, the United Nations, OSCE, European Union (EU) and other Non- Governmental Organizations (NGO's). All that and plus make daily reports to the Chief of Border Police at the border headquarters in Pristina. Our final objective was to train and mentor the newly established local border police staff.

All of the international staff stationed in-county lived in rented or lease housing in their respective assigned regions. We were assigned to the Prizren region and found housing within the city of Prizren. Prizren is one of the oldest cities in the Balkans. The region had a heavy Turkish influence. Many of the citizens were Albanian and Turkish decent. A Gorani population was represented as well but mostly living in the mountain area. The Gorani people were basically Muslims who spoke a Slavic language. During my tour at the Vrbnica border, I would drive to the Goran villages in the mountains and visit. The Gorani people were known for their pastries and their home brew Rakki. Rakki is a popular alcohol drink made from plums or grapes.

In the center of Prizren, was a shopping district called Shadervan. It was a place surrounded by beautiful mountains and within the Shadevan, restaurants and shops. Every evening the center was busy with people walking around and/or sitting at an outside coffee shop. We would often visit the Turkish restaurants, sit outside, and enjoy a meal and a calm evening.

●

As mentioned, one of my duties was to liaison with NATO personnel. In these meetings we were to come up with innovating ideas to help build schools and improve the living conditions in the villages surrounding the border. On one such meeting, I met with a US Marine colonel who was the Liaison officer between NATO and the UN. The Colonel who I will call Colonel, came to the border station and asked if I would accompany him to the village of Vrbnica. The colonel was trying to get the village only water pump that supplied the village with fresh drinking water, working again. We visited the village and met with the village elders. After the meeting the Colonel asked me to join him for lunch in Prizren. We went to the Shadervan area and sat outside in the shade at a Turkish restaurant. The Shadervan area was busy with pedestrians walking and enjoying the warm afternoon. It was about 1100 hours (11 am for you civilians). We sat and discussed on how we were going to attack the problem of the village broken pump. We had lunch and decided to drink a cool Peje draft beer. We sat and discussed for quite awhile until it was time for dinner. The colonel and I, who by that time were both on first name basis. He called me Bob and I called him Colonel. The Marine in me never left as far as respect goes. We were at the restaurant for a full 8 hours discussing the plight of

Kosovo, the plight of the world, the Marine Corps and the possibility of him or me becoming mayor of Prizren and having beers named after us.

We eventually did get the village pump working with the aid of NATO resources. The colonel and remained friends and often visited several villages to assist the locals in any way we could.

•

At one point, I was called into Border HQ and asked if I was up to the task of looking over the building of two additional border crossing station. One in the mountain village of Kristac that bordered Albania and the other at the Kosovo/Macedonia border near the mountain village of Restilica (pronounced Resteliza) I agreed to oversee this task after being assured we would get proper logistics and staff.

After several months of wheeling and dealing with the UN and UNMIK the border stations were finally built and staffed. I enjoyed traveling to the Restelica border station. The mountains and hills were covered with grass and several sheep farms were scattered throughout the area. Several while visiting the Restelica BCP eagles could be seen soaring overhead. Even the staff of Border HQ enjoyed traveling to the Restelica BCP.

Don't Do It Bob

On several occasions I had the opportunity to enjoy the city life with several of my comrades and/or staff. Particularly my German colleagues. One evening after work several of us decided to meet for dinner and go out for drinks. That usually meant skipping dinner and just having drinks. My Deputy Commander, a German colleague I will call Kai, my Chief of Operations Joe, my best friend and language assistant (LA) Noli and several more international officers decided to drive to a beautiful mountainous city called Djakova (pronounced Jakova). Some may consider it a village.

This was on a Friday evening and we had heard of a party going on in Djakova, We piled into 3 separate vehicles, UN and Coca Cola's (red and white Toyota Police marked vehicle). I was driving the lead white UN Toyota 4 Runner. Kai was behind me in a Coca Cola and the rest followed. I can say this now and not fear of being 'Repatriated' back to the states, but we also had a couple of the local women (no not painted ladies) with us in our official vehicle. I prefer to think of it as my civic duty.

So on we went to Djakova for fun and adventure. After we arrived we went to an extra-large building that had been made into a night club. A lot of the local residents were in there having a good time. The music could be heard from outside of the building. 'Oh this will be fun'. After approximately 2 hours some gun shots that sounded like an AK 47, were heard coming from outside the club. People began running back into the club. We gathered everyone that came with us, I quickly made a head count to ensure we were all there and decided to go back to Prizren. We got back into our vehicles, Did I mentioned we were all armed? Yes all my staff were armed as this was still considered a war zone. Anyway we headed to Prizren in a hurry.

Upon reaching the city of Prizren, I could see blue lights flashing down the road in front of me. Traffic was at a standstill and I drove around it towards the blue flashing lights. Kai was in the vehicle behind me and followed. As I reached the scene, I saw several local (Kosovo Police) vehicles with their blue emergency lights on. The first thing I see is a large Kosovo Albanian slap one of the local police officers. Upon being slapped in the face by this civilian the Kosovo Police and his partners did not take any action. I immediately jumped out to assist this officer.

I later was told by Kai that he had seen me stop and he too saw what had happened but did not think we should of gotten involved because we all had been drinking. He told me when I had stopped he knew what was going to happen and he kept saying *"don't do it Bob, don't do it Bob"*. Well I did it.

I approached the officers and asked why is this suspect still standing and not on the ground in handcuffs. The KPS officer told me "it's no problem" and the suspect was leaving. Since we (UNMIK Police) were still under executive powers and the Rule of Law, I gave him an order to arrest the suspect. The KPS officer just stood there and stared at me. The suspect started to walk away from the scene. The suspect was about 6'5" and well over 200 pounds? As he walked away, I ran to him and jumped on his neck area with a head lock and let my momentum carry us to the asphalt. As we came to the ground, I used my right hand to break the fall and I heard it go 'crunch'. By that time, Kai, Joe and the rest of the staff came to assist in putting handcuffs on the suspect. The suspect was taken into custody by the KPS Tac team.

The following morning, I visited the German military hospital in Prizren where my hand was x-rayed. I was told I had three fractures in my wrist. Anyway no pain, no pain.

After I returned to the border station I filed a report to the Chief of KPS and to our border HQ. Internal Affairs officers came to visit later that day. The KPS officer who did not take action after being slapped was later dismissed. I was relieved nothing was mentioned about us having partaking in the consumption of alcohol that evening.

We later found out the reason the suspect was not arrested by the KPS, He was allegedly a member of the Albanian Mafia and a member of a criminal organization called the Black Panthers or something to that effect. The KPS officer feared for his life and that of his family because this organization was known in the trafficking of women, arms and narcotics.

Part of our duties as border police was to investigate the trafficking of humans. We assisted KFOR troops in raiding several bars known to traffic women. Many arrest were made and the victims turned over to the proper UN agencies. Some of the young female victims, whom many were from former Soviet Union countries would tell us they had been sold by family members or kidnapped. Raids such as these were done while we were heavily armed.

•

As an International Police officer, I had the occasion to travel throughout Europe on my time off. I was taking a flight to Barcelona Spain for the weekend and we had a three hour layover in Ljubljana, Slovenia. We disembarked the plane and were directed to Passport Control so we could wait in the airport lobby. I was waiting in line for my turn to passport control. While in line an airport police officer grabbed me from my arm and told me to come with him. I instantly began thinking if I had remembered to leave my weapon in Kosovo or if it was in my back pack I was carrying. The police officer didn't say much as he escorted me to a room with a table in the center and wall lockers lining the room.

In the center of this room are a table and a couple of chairs. The airport police officer told me to take a seat and he left the room closing the door behind him. I was about to check my back pack to make sure I left my duty weapon behind. The door suddenly opens and two Slovenian officers walk in. I immediately recognized them as colleagues who were assigned to my border station in Kosovo months prior. They both shouted "Commander" and gave me a big hug. One of them went to a wall locker, opened it and brought out a bottle of Slovenian Rakki. That was some powerful hooch but smooth. For the almost three hours I had to wait until my departure, we sat in that room and finished the bottle of Rakki. When it came time for me to leave they literally had to help me on the plane and told the flight crew that I was to sit in first class. Most travelers worried about airport police while traveling abroad. I worried about meeting officers I worked with and they would get me drunk before flying. That happened in another airport as well.

•

Running on the border

Almost every day after work, I would change into my Marine Corps PT gear including combat boots and begin my daily run along the river Drini that flowed south passing our border station and into Albania. I always enjoyed running on a small trail I found along the river. Before starting the run, I would get my Marine K-Bar knife secured in its sheath and place it in my waist band behind my back.

I often ran 4 to 5 miles and then head back to the border. Like I had mentioned, the trail ran along the river and it was below eye level from the main roadway. I enjoyed the stillness and fresh cool air. At times the dam located about 80 miles south into Albania was closed and it would cause the river to back up thus creating a lake blocking my jogging trail.

Being the Old Jarhead (Marine), I would not detour from my 'mission'; I'd simply dive in and swim to where the trail began again, get out and continue with the run. On one particular run, I heard a German military patrol calling to me from the main roadway. The German patrol also called German KFOR had the responsibility of protecting the region and our border Area of Responsibility (AOR). I ran up the bank onto the roadway where KFOR soldiers were. The German sergeant said to me "*Commander, do you know you are running in a mine field?*" "*That area has not been cleared of mines yet*". This area of the border was one of the most heavily mine fields. I never ran that trail again, however I did find another nice trail alongside the mountain.

•

At the border station, the Chief of KPS was an American I will call John. John was in his early 60s and at that time I was 50 or thereafter. John was in good shape and liked to run as well. John and I discussed the possibility of running the dirt roadway on the Restilica border. As mentioned before and if you did not skip that chapter you would know the village of Restilica was literally in the mountains along the Macedonia border.

We decided to run that trail on a Saturday and with the assistance of another American who at the time was the Chief of Operation, would follow us in a vehicle to provide any assistance should we keel over. The following Saturday John and I ran the trail. The day was perfect, sunny, and cool. I recall the air was thin as it became a struggle to breathe while running. I believe we ran at least 10 miles that day. As you can imaging, the down slopes were easy but the up hills were a Blankity Blank (insert your words here). Anyway we made it without any major issues. Thanks John.

Dr. Bob

The contractor we were working for made provision to provide a Medic to each of the regions we were assigned. The Medics provided our personnel with any medical assistance whenever any emergency came up. If the emergency was sever, then arraignments were made to be medi-vac (medical evacuation) out.

At the time, we had an active duty US Army Special Forces medic, who had taken his remaining leave from the Army to contract with our company, before his retirement. I will call him "Doc".

Doc and I had become close friends, on occasion we would take extended weekends and visit other countries to unwind. More about that later.

One evening, I was attempting to punch an extra hole in my belt, since I had lost some weight and needed to tighten up the belt. I was using a folding knife I had purchased in the base PX at Camp Bondsteel. While holding the belt, the knife slipped and sliced right into the little finger of my left hand. Oh, did I make mention that I has been drinking? Well I was. Anyway, I immediately applied pressure and said a few choice words questioning my intelligence. The bleeding would not stop. I dug around my bags and found a sewing needle with various colors of thread. I chose the green spool of thread since it reminded me of Marine green. After several attempts to thread the needle, I finally accomplished that. I sewed two beautiful stiches to close the wound. By the way I was still drinking to ease the pain. Hey one uses what one has. After admiring my handy stich work. I cleaned it and wrapped the finger.

The next three days, I could feel the finger pulsating with pain. On the 4th day, I finally went to see Doc. After unwrapping the bandage, my finger was about 3 times its size and almost black.

Doc lovingly jerked the almost unseen stiches out and unleashed a barrage words I hadn't heard since boot camp. Brought tears to my eyes (sniff). Something about I could have lost my blanking finger and I was a blanking idiot and blankity blank this and blankity blank that. He was after my heart. It was fun and games until Doc commenced to scrub and clean my finger. Now real tears, ouch. After Doc was done cleaning the wound, he patted me on the head, made the sign of the cross and sent me on my way.

•

Vampires in Kukes

On many occasions, I had the opportunity to meet with members of the Organization for the Security and Cooperation of Europe (OSCE). One in particular was Gabi, a Romanian who was assigned to the OSCE office in Kukes Albania. Kukes is located in the northern border of Albania with Kosovo. It lies at the foothill of Vikut and Gjalica mountains. Its population at the time was around 15,000 inhabitants.

The OSCE maintained a beautiful villa that overlooked a lake the Fierza reservoir. On occasion, Gabi would visit our border for meetings and invite us to the villa for a weekend. One weekend I accepted her invitation.

It was on a Friday evening, the air was cool and we were outside cooking on a grill and having 'refreshments'. Gabi had some friends visit from Romania. They worked for the OSCE as well, an often spend the weekend at this beautiful place. We were all sitting outside when her guest, who by the way were husband and wife, mentioned they were actually from the Transylvania region of Romania. The discussion that afternoon went into Count Dracula and/or Vlad the Impaler. The Romanian guest were very nice and spoke perfect English but I detected an accent you might hear in a Dracula movie. As the sun went down and the food was ready, we went into the villa to get ourselves ready for dinner. The villa is a three story beautiful building with balconies on each floor overlooking the lake.

As we went inside, I sidestepped to the kitchen and found the aluminum foil. I tore off a large piece and went upstairs to my room. While in my room, I fashioned a large cross out of the aluminum foil. I found a string of garlic as well and took that to my room. Gabi later called us down stairs for dinner. I was already seated at the dining table when the other guest arrived. My two new friends from Romania came down the stairs at the same time that was next to the dining room and the first thing they see is me, sitting at the dining table with a big silver colored cross hanging from my shirt and a string of garlic around my neck. As if on que, when they saw me they turned their heads away from me and said "remove that cross". We had a good laugh. I however, upon retiring to my room, took the cross to hang on my bedroom door just in case.

•

As part of our duties with UNMIK, we had to mentor the new established Kosovo Police. At our border station UNMIK began allowing Kosovo Police Commanders in the station to learn the system and eventually take over the station. One of the Kosovo Border Police commanders was a female Lt Colonel who was to shadow me on the day to day operation of the border. Later in 2011 she was to become the newly elected President of the Republic of Kosovo. I was honored to meet and work with her.

•

The time spent in Kosovo, I had the privilege of meeting and working with many international police officers. These memories and friendship will last forever. Special thanks go to Noli and his beautiful family. Noli was our language assistant but most importantly he became a friend and brother. A lot of us spent the holidays away from our families but the Toci family took us in and made us family during these lonely times.

•

As I've mentioned before and if you were paying attention, we were under the United Nations Mission in Kosovo (UNMIK) a pillar of the United Nations. All the logistics required for our daily operations on the border and other departments were supplied by UNMIK. The United Nations had their own logistics command in Kosovo to supply the other UN pillars in country. One such UN Log base was in the city of Prizren at a place known as Printex. The UN employee in charge of the Log base was a short bald man from Ireland. I will call him Patrick. I was told several times to not ask Patrick for anything and to go through our own UNMIK logistics for supplies. I heard from several persons that Patrick was probably the meanest person in Kosovo and stay out of his way. Several times while walking past his office, I would hear him shouting obscenities at someone over the phone. Keep all this in mind readers as you read on.

At our border station we were in the process of adding two other border crossing points and UNMIK was slow in providing logistics such as vehicles and other materials. My Chief of Operations, Joe, who happened to be a former co-worker at Hidalgo PD and a friend and I decided to jump the chain of command (I've been known to do that often) and ask the UN for vehicles. I believed we needed three at the time. We were trying to figure out a plan to talk to Patrick without him throwing us out the second floor window.

One evening Joe and I are in town at a local establishment (Noli's Bar) frequent by UNMIK personnel. We saw Patrick sitting at a table by himself. I asked the bar tender what type of drink Patrick was ordering and told him to send him a round on me. Patrick accepted it and invited us to sit at the table with him. Joe and I sat, bought him rounds and he returned the favor. Soon we were enjoying ourselves singing and laughing. Patrick said something that sounded like "you lads are ok, anything you need come by my office". Well, that is what I wanted to hear. Prior to leaving, we hugged and exchanged decoders' rings. We promised to do this again. We hit pay dirt.

A couple of days later, Joe and I were in the Printex building to see Patrick. While walking the hallway towards his office, I could hear shouting and cursing coming from Patrick's office. I was thinking to myself that maybe this was not a right time or good idea. At the entrance we were met by Patrick's secretary who escorted us to his office. At the door way Patrick looks up and invited us in. He was glad to see us. He asked what we were doing there and I explained our dilemma of acquiring vehicles from UNMIK for our border patrol officer's. He said something that sounded like "F*** UNMIK, call me in a few days". After a couple of days we had 3 brand new Land Rovers delivered to our station.

Wait readers, it didn't just end there. After the vehicles arrived, I was called in to UNMIK HQ (headquarters) for a "meeting". When I arrived, I was met by the Chief of UNMIK Logistics and some other third world persons who were trying very hard to intimidate me. They said something about I had no right in going over their heads and the rest I heard was blah blah blah, I could be repatriated, blah blah blah. This conversation was getting boring I responded by saying if they needed to say anything to me or tried to reprimand me they would have to follow the chain of command and speak to the Chief of Border Police and not me (interesting, I was citing the chain of command now). They did not like it and asked me to leave. OK, F you very much see you later. By the way, at that time my Chief of Border Police (my boss) was a German Colonel with the famed GSG9 who liked my style of running the border station and self-initiative. The Grenzschutzgruppe 9 or GSG9 are the German counter-terrorism special operations of the Federal Border Police (Bundesgrenzschutz). A great bunch of operators I had the pleasure of working with and putting a few rounds down range. Never challenge them in any drinking contest either.

•

After the war, Kosovo was littered with unexploded ordinance (land mines). Occasionally, some local villagers would walk up to the border station carrying land mines that were found while they were farming their land. Even children had walked up carrying anti-tank mines.

•

Our Albanian counterparts on the other side of our border station were having a ceremony for their new border building at the crossing point. It was my understanding the US government assisted in the funding of the building. Several dignitaries including the Albanian Prime Minister, Fatos Nano and the US Counselor were present. The ceremony was completed and the dignitaries were asked to join the final festivities upstairs in the new border building. I turned around and began walking across the border when one of the Prime Minister's security team members stopped me and told me that Mr Nano wanted me to join them upstairs. I went up and as I walked in the conference room, I was handed a tall glass of Gin and

Mineral water with ice. The security member that handed me the glass told me Mr. Nano wanted to visit with me. I walked over to where the Prime Minister was standing, talking to some of the guest. He saw me and motioned me to the bar area. He had the bartender give us two more drinks of Gin and water. After a short discussion about the situation on the border, Mr. Nano asked if I would allow his staff to cross the border to visit a well-known fish restaurant in the village of Vrbnica. I told Mr. Nano, I would do better than that and I would escort them myself.

The Prime Minister's staff with part of the security team and I went to the fish restaurant up the road from our border station. The restaurant had live trout in a pool next to the building. The cold water that is being fed into the pool was diverted from the mountain by use of manmade canals. The waiters would take nets, catch the trout and the cooks would bake or grill it for you. As we waited, several bottles of wine were brought to our table. After the fine meal, I asked for the bill but was told by the manager that the bill had been taken care of by the Prime Minister.

•

On several occasions the Vrbnica border crossing played host to Prime Ministers and dignitaries from several countries represented within the United Nations. We were visited constantly as well by members of the OSCE and EU representatives. The Vrbnica border station was at the time, the largest border crossing on the northern Albanian border. We hosted monthly meetings as well with our Albanian counterparts and NATO personnel. I was constantly reminded by each of my Deputy Commanders and Chief of Operations to let them handle the daily operations of the borders stations (of there were three) and I should handle the meeting aspects. It was because of my staff, that I looked good to the chiefs at HQ. They made me look good because of the good job they did. I, on the other hand, looked forward to getting in my vehicle and patrol the border and visit the various villages. I did not care for being in the office if I didn't have to be. My Administrative Assistant Zihnie took excellent care of all the paper work and did an outstanding job of reminding me of meetings and appointments. She and the other female staff were bringing home cooked meals as well. I guess that was the reason why I ran a lot.

Several times, UNMIK HQ would attempt to down size my local staff. I would make the argument, since I was the only commander in country in charge of more than one border station, we needed all the staff, local and international. This would cause the downsizing to be placed on hold. My staff spoke up for the KPS several times. We even got extra help. We spoke up for the local staff because these people were relying on this job to feed their families. There were no other jobs to be had other than working for the UN or NATO as language assistance. We always knew one day it would end and they would have to seek employment elsewhere but, I promised them as long as I could, they would have a job at the station.

We even had to take up for our Kosovo Border Police officers assigned to our station. It seemed UNMIK and KPS (Kosovo Police Service) were sending their local officers from northern Kosovo way down south to our border station. Many didn't have a way to make it to the border. Some had to pay to take a bus or taxi. The local officers were making the equivalent of $130 a month to feed their families. I asked KPS HQ to provide us with vehicles their police officers could get to work and back. That was turned down. I will say that many KPS of higher ranks in the capital had new vehicles assigned to them, while my officers had to ride four or five in a single vehicle just to patrol. UNMIK HQ and KPS HQ didn't like to see me walking up to their office. At times, the international staff would pay the KPS officer's bus fare out of their own pocket. We would always argue for more equipment or pay for my officers. Our border HQ knew how I was when it came to my station and officers so they let me do my thing as long as I didn't shoot anyone or throw someone out the window. We had an outstanding crew.

The KPS Border Police at our station were always making good seizures of narcotics or weapons. They worked hard and were appreciative of everything we as international staff did for them. I was not the only one working hard for these people. I personally observed international police officers from other nations care just as much as I did. They believed in the mission we were tasked with. Like I mentioned before, we were police officers in our home countries and may be from different parts of the globe but the feeling and caring of being a police officer was the same. When I would get bored doing paperwork in my office, I would go out to the lines at the check point and check vehicles along with passengers. The KPS that were on break would come out, take the passport I was holding and tell me that I was the commander and should not be on the lines. I did that many times as motivation for the KPS.

In my very last day as Commander of the Vrbnica border, the international staff took down the UN flag from the flag pole, signed it and presented it to me. The local staff brought in food and drinks and we held a teary goodbye. I will always be grateful to each of them.

•

Group 4

After the end of my Kosovo/UNMIK contract, I returned to the states, I was there a few months before I got another contract with the US Department of Defense through a company out of the United Kingdom. The contract was to provide security for US military installations. This job was in Kosovo at US Army base, Camp Bonsteel. Our duties were to provide perimeter security and check all vehicles entering the base for any contraband or improvised explosive devise (IEDs). Each team or shift had approximately 10 to 12 armed officers assigned to different location of the base. I usually volunteered to work the main gate as 'over watch'. My duties as over watch were to provide security over the main gate officer checking identification on all military and nonmilitary personnel entering the base. We were situated above the main gate office with an M16, making sure all vehicles came to a complete stop at a designated point. I did that work for about a year and rotated back to the states. I would say without incident but since it was a DOD contract I will leave it like that.

•

At Camp Bondsteel there were few of us that were prior police officers in the states and even fewer who had already been deployed to Kosovo with UNMIK. The project manager of the base security team was a former UNMIK police officer and a friend. We previously served together in

Kosovo. Under contract with DOD, the rules and regulations were strict. We were not allowed to live off base (eventually I did). We were not allowed to drink any alcohol while in country, especially on the base (guilty as charge). Any violation of the policies could get someone repatriated, meaning sent home.

Many of the security members had been in the military and deployed to both Iraq and Afghanistan. One particular individual was trying hard to be liked by the rest of the team. He bragged a lot about his tour in Iraq with the US Army and how he won the bronze star. I thought to myself, good for him. I would speak to him now and then while on duty. He would try to get the others to laugh by making fun of my stuttering. I have had to asked him several time not to do that and made it known to him I did not care for it. On one particular afternoon, we had gotten off shift and were in the armory turning in our weapons and ammo. He started making fun of me, attempting to get the others to laugh. He was standing directly behind me and without thinking, I grabbed him from the throat, Marine Drill Instructor style and punched him in the face and threw him on the floor. Immediately, upon seeing that, the rest of the team got me off of him and several supervisors came in. When asked what happened, I didn't say anything and walked out. I had it in my mind I was being sent home so I went to the sea hut to pack my gear. The project manager and his assistant came to the sea hut where I was living and asked what had happened. I gave them the details and they apologized to me for what had happened. The project manager asked if I would want for them to send this idiot home. I told them it was not necessary as long as he quit what he was doing. They agreed and left. Later that evening, that individual came to my living quarters to apologize for what happened. Some of the other team members came to me and said they did not blame me for what I did and were wondering why I had not done this earlier.

•

After leaving Kosovo at the end of my contract I was between deployments and looking for work state side. I got hired as a security team leader and advisor for a government contracted plant that packaged Meals Ready to Eat (MRE's) for the US military. This plant was located in south Texas at the time. Getting hired by the company post 9/11 was a chore in itself. Anyway, I got on with the company and quickly made some new friends. One of the managers for the company, I will call Jerrell and I became good friends. One morning we were standing in front of the building talking among ourselves and nearby to us was the Human Resource (HR) lady appearing not to listen to our conversation. Jarrell and I were joking around and I mentioned the word "white boy". This lady almost choked on her cigarette when she heard me. She immediately came to where we were standing and said something to the effect that I should not use that word as it was improper and sounded racist. Jerrell, immediately said to me, *"Yea Bob, don't you know we are the Master Race you should have more respect for us"*. We both broke into a laughter as the HR lady again choked on her cigarette. Even I was not expecting that. I thought it was funny and on time.

Languages

I have always maintained the knack for languages. Growing up I had a bad speech impediment that required me to not speak to anyone if I didn't have too. I recall a teacher I had in grade school who intentionally made fun of it and allowed the class to laugh at me. The majority of the time I kept to myself and tried not to be called out to read anything in front of the class. I kind of broke out of that when I joined the Marine Corps. When I would deployed to different countries I would pay close attention to the different languages spoken in whichever foreign soil I happened to be in. It helped that I spoke Spanish and some French. While I was attending Hampton University and working as a campus police officer, one of the university professors invited me to attend her speech pathology class. I learned to control my speech patterns.

Becoming a police officer forced me to control my speech and received the confidence to continue with my job. While at the Hidalgo Police department, our chief assigned me to attend the instructor's course at Texas A&M in College Station. I went to the chief and asked not to be sent to the class. I explained why I didn't want to attend and the chief's words to me were, *"what speech problem, you don't have a speech problem. You are going to the class"*. I knew during the course of training, the students would have to give short class of instructions in front of the class. It would be video recorded. I attended the course and eventually attended the advanced course. As an instructor I assisted in teaching the Hidalgo High School law enforcement class. At the police department, I initiated the Hidalgo Police Training Center and got it approved by the Texas Commission of Law Enforcement Officers Standards and Education (TCLOSE) of which I was lead instructor.

After, deployment to Kosovo, I found, I could pick up languages quite easily. I would ask our local Language Assistants (LA's) to teach me certain phrases. These, I would write down to memorize. Eventually I would mixed the words and phrases. Working side by side with international police officers, I would asked to learned phrases or words of several languages. I picked up Turkish, Russian, French, Polish, Twi (Ghana dialect) plus Albanian. I concentrated more on the Albanian language. During my tour, I would take trips to different European nations and practice my language skills; France was probably the hardest country to practice my skills since many of the French didn't care too much for Americans. Once, while in La Rochelle France, I switch my French to a Spanish accent and was asked by a local vendors if I was Basque. That worked for me.

I got to where I could recognize the different accents in the Albanian language. I could recognize the different regions of where Albanians would come from. The ethnic Albanians in Macedonia, Kosovo and Albania each had a particular accent. We had an incident on the border when an Albanian citizen was attempting to enter Kosovo without travel documents. He had told the international border officer he was from Kosovo. I arrived to assist and I asked where he was from. The person told me he was from Prizren Kosovo. I recognized he was speaking Albanian in an accent of the northern Albania region of Haas. I told the officer to refuse the entrance. A language assistant later confirmed that the person was in fact from the Haas region and asked how I knew this.

CHAPTER IV

Narcotics Agent

Undercover Operations

Upon my return to the United Stated, I journeyed back to the Rio Grande Valley of deep south Texas. My intention was to get back into police work and settle down. I wanted to be near my kids as I lost a lot of time away from them. I hand delivered resumes at various police departments in the area. In a couple of the departments, after reviewing my resume, I was actually told I could not be hired because of fear I would take their jobs. Two of these officers were in ranking positions within their respective departments. After gaining employment in New Mexico, I later found that these same individual officers had been indicted for narcotics trafficking. Hmmm, I wonder why I was not wanted in South Texas. Not being able to find employment in south Texas I relocated to New Mexico.

Hobbs, New Mexico is usually known as or called Hobbs America. After arriving in Hobbs, I was immediately hired as an undercover (UC) agent with the Lea County Drug Task Force. Prior to this, I had never worked undercover but I eagerly accepted the challenge. I looked forward to the adrenaline rush I would encounter. The hiring process was quite extensive as I had to quickly get certified as a police officer by the state of New Mexico. My undercover status caused me and the city of Hobbs to complete my physical, psychological and any other exam in the neighboring state of Texas. Documents I had to sign were also completed across the state line in Texas. The reason for this was so no one locally, would know that an undercover agent had been hired. Even the local police did not know who I was. I was even hired under an alias name for pay and record purposes. Since I had to create an undercover identity, I was provided with a driver's license and social security number under my newly created name other than the other alias I was hired under. In other words, I had two aliases. Both first names were Jimmy but the last names were different.

In my undercover capacity, I used Santiago Nichols. Santiago is Spanish for James; therefore I was known by many as "Jimmy". I used that particular name not only because that was my mother's grandfather's name but because it kind of threw the bad guys off as far as made up names go. In this part of the country, there are a lot of Mennonites from Mexico that are of German decent. They have German or Dutch surnames. On one of the case reports made by an ICE/HSI Special Agent, he wrote while interrogating a suspect, the suspect told him that he sold the methamphetamine to a 'Guedo' (pronounced Wedo/white guy) that spoke very good Spanish. I recall that case, the bad guy thought I was Mennonite. To this day, even after retirement I am called Jimmy by those that were not in the drug scene but whom I had met during my UC work.

I had to create a fictional biography starting with my year of birth, the type of jobs I have had. I would always have to use the same information and remember it. Some times during long term undercover operations, someone would think they are good friends with you and want to know more about you and your background. I told everyone I was medically retired from the Marine Corps and was now doing day work on different ranches. I would have to stick with that story. I could not tell anyone that I was working in the oil field and not know anything about it. When the issue of why I was into selling drugs was ever discussed with the bad guys, I would say that the VA doesn't give me enough to provide for an ex-wife and a yard full of kids. They often would buy that story. As an undercover, you are always being scrutinized by the bad guys looking for some tell tail sign you might be a police officer.

Often I carried a prescription bottle of real heart medication, prescribed by a trusted Pharmacist made out to my undercover name in case I was asked to do a line of cocaine or hit the meth pipe. I would simply say I was in it for the money and could not use anything because of my heart problem. At times I would break into preaching to the bad guy, telling them that, the reason drug dealers always got caught was because they would use their own product. Many would agree with that analogy.

It is believed by many that undercover agents have to do narcotics to prove to the bad guys, we are bad guys as well. That is not always the case. First, it is dangerous, second it is illegal and you could be criminally charged just as much as the bad guy. You may lose your case in a trial.

I have been asked by many attorneys in court if I have tried the product, referring to cocaine or methamphetamine. They want us to say yes. The case is lost right then. I will add, the only time an agent would want to do it is, if their life depended on it. A scenario would have to be, if I was in the middle of an undercover buy and was forced to try it. Thank God, I was never in that situation.

On one undercover purchase, I was in a barn with several suspects. I was purchasing a couple of pounds of cocaine. The cocaine was kept in a large plastic bag in a barrel. Yes they had a lot. The bad guy scooped some into a plastic bag for me and stuck his finger in the cocaine. He pulled his finger out and stuck it into his mouth. He said it was good stuff and asked me to try it. Two of the other bad guys were behind me and the one who told me to taste it was standing right next to me. I knew right then I didn't have much of a choice and could not think of anything to say at that point. I swiftly stuck my right index finger into the bag of the white powdery substance and stuck my middle finger in my mouth. I recall doing it in a fast motion. I brought my hand down and wiped my index finger with the cocaine residue on my pants. I quickly began talking to the bad guy about something else to draw his attention from what I just did. It seemed to work. On TV, you see where the so called agent or police officer stick a finger and taste the cocaine. Again that is a huge mistake. One really doesn't know what is in it. By tasting it, you may be putting something other than cocaine in your mouth. So no, in the real world no agent rubs their gum with cocaine or anything else.

To me, cocaine smells like wet dirt. It's a kind of scent you get after a rain shower on soil. That is what it smells like to me. Several agents have said the same thing.

When one is working undercover and spending a lot of time with the bad guys you have to always be alert and quick with responses. It took me awhile to get to that point. I tried not to get too comfortable when I am around them, however I did not want to always seem nervous. The times I appeared to be nervous, I played it as if I was just nervous about being busted by the police.

As an undercover, especially a buy bust operation or short term operation, I would not allow myself to give out too much information about my background. I would give them my first name only and make the buy (drug purchase). Many times when the bad guys didn't know you they would get curious and start asking questions trying to figure who you are. If I was purchasing small amounts of drugs, I would take the buy money out of my pocket or wherever it was kept and the bad guy would focus on the money. On one such operation, I actually, accidently, took my badge out of my pocket during the buy. I was in this bad guy's house buying a couple of rocks of crack cocaine for $40.00. I have never made it a habit of carrying anything resembling law enforcement as an undercover. I do not know or recall why the badge was in my pocket but never the less it was there. While talking to the bad guy I had the $40.00 dollars in my right hand. The bad guy never took his eyes off the money.

With my left hand I reached into my pocket to retrieve my vehicle's keys. I felt the badge and not thinking it was the badge, I pulled it out of my pocket and looked at it. The bad guy was standing directly in front of me at the time. My heart skipped a beat several times and I quickly put the badge back. The bad guy, never saw the badge I held in my left hand. His full attention was on the money I was holding in my right hand. I am such an idiot. Never the less, the transaction went down without incident.

•

The task force I was assigned to, was comprised of agents from the Lea County Sheriff's department and officers from the surrounding cities of Hobbs, Lovington, Eunice and Tatum police departments. From the very beginning these agents made me feel right at home. Being the new guy. I became the recipient of narcotics agent's practical jokes. In agencies around the country, no matter how large or small, there is a comradery among its officers or agents. A real brotherhood. These are the people we trust with our lives. However, narcotics agents are notorious for their practical jokes. In my time with the task force, I had coffee creamer put in my vehicle's air condition vents (Kemp), grape jelly on my windshield wipers and so on. We each had a tough job to do and did it well, but on down time it seemed chaotic. Whenever I went on vacation, I learned to keep my undercover vehicle locked when it was stored in the bay,

The Pecos Valley Drug Task Force was no different when I worked there as a narcotics agent. Even the federal agents were not immune to pranks from our agents as you will later read.

•

My first undercover drug buy, I was nervous. I have never worked undercover except a short stint while working a vice detail in Dallas. On this my first buy, I was provided with $40.00 of drug task force contingency funds. The plan was for me meet with a confidential informant (CI). The CI was to take me to a known crack dealer's residence and introduce me to him. As in all operations, a surveillance team always followed me to keep me under surveillance, thus keeping me safe. I was wearing a miniature recorder I kept in my pocket.

The CI and I drove up to the known crack dealer's residence southeast of town. While walking to the door, I recall having all kinds of thoughts going through my head. I've never worked undercover but I had seen movies so I was expecting the worst. I worried if I was going to be asked to do the drug in front of them, to prove I was not a cop. Anyway we made contact with this known crack dealer and we were invited in the house. The house was an old A frame house with minimal furniture. The CI and the suspect talked for a few minutes and finally the CI told him I was a friend and I wanted to "get hooked up with a couple of rocks". The suspect invited us to a back bedroom and told me to sit on the bed. I could feel my heart pumping double time but I tried to remain calm. After I sat down, the crack dealer took a metal type pipe and lit the contents that were in the small bowl at the end of the pipe. I now began thinking he is going to offer me a hit off the pipe. By law, I knew I was not allowed to do any drugs to prove I was not the police. I was trying very hard to remain calm and not panic. The crack dealer sat next to me calmly smoking the crack cocaine. He asked me several questions about who I was and the kind of work I did. I had told him I was new in the Hobbs area and owned a yard service company. He never did ask me to hit the pipe. I was glad to recognize crack heads didn't like to share their product.

After finishing the crack cocaine, the crack dealer handed me 2 small yellowish colored rocks. I examined the rocks pretending I knew what I was doing. I really did not. The CI jumped in and said "Its cool". I placed the crack rocks in my shirt pocket and handed the suspect the money. I felt a great deal of joy knowing I made my first undercover purchase. I was thinking, the rest was going to be easy. Little did I know what was in store for me?

Leaving the residence, I began feeling the adrenaline running in me. I was still nervous as this was my very first purchase. I remember thinking that perhaps the bad guy might follow me to see if I was a police officer. I began thinking paranoid thoughts. As I was driving back to the task force, I looked in my rear view mirror and noticed an old model white pickup following me. I had not recognized that pickup truck at the task force so it caused me to think that the bad guy was following me. I was beginning to wonder where was my surveillance? Did they take another route back to the task force? Why was this truck following me? Many thoughts were going through my head.

I decided to turn at different intersections to shake this person that appeared to be following me. I drove a couple of blocks and made a right turn, then drive a couple of more blocks and turn again. The person following me was doing the same by staying close behind me. I really started to get nervous by then. I made up my mind to just drive to the task force office and hope to catch one of the agents who should be arriving by the time I got there. As I neared the task force I noticed this person was still following me. I arrived at the front of the task force office and the white pickup parked right next to me. It was then that I saw who had been tailing me. It was the State Police sergeant assigned to the task force. I had not recognized the older model pickup he had been driving. This entire time I thinking the bad guy was following me or had sent someone. I was very much relieved.

•

Undercover duty involved going out to different locations where criminals or "bad guys" were known to hang out. Occasionally I was to meet and attempt to purchase narcotics from anyone who would sell to me. Every place I visited as part of my duties, such as a bar, restaurant or any place where the public hangs out. As I entered an establishment I would scan the place and profile future suspects. I then would initiate conversation with a potential suspect; the conversation would begin about any topic other than drugs. Often I would wait until asked what kind of work I was into. I'd begin by saying I was medically retire from the Marine Corps. I would then ad, I use to sell cocaine but had to quit because things were heating up for me. I would then change the subject and talk about something else. If the person was paying attention and involved in the drug game he or she would bring up the subject again. If they didn't then they were not interested and not involved or were worried I was not the person who I said I was.

The bars were always my best locations to meet new contacts. I have worked biker bars, cantinas, casinos and sports bars. Most likely than not I would hit pay dirt. I would begin conversation with someone, buy them a few rounds of drinks and bring up the subject of whatever kind of narcotics I was looking for.

When going into a new place, like a bar, I begin by starting a semi friendship with a bartender or waitress. I did this because they knew everything that goes on in the bar area and knew most of the regular customer. The other reason for meeting the bartender or waitress first, so any potential suspect would see me talking and laughing with the bartender and I would hope they would think I was a regular customer.

Once I felt that the bartender got comfortable with me, I would bring up the subject of me wanting to purchase some narcotics. (No, I would not ask to buy 'narcotics'. We had a joke in the task force about me asking a dealer if they would sell me "Schedule II Narcotics". That is the terminology given by the FDA and DEA). Anyway, depending how comfortable I got in the establishment I was in, I would let the bartender know I was interested in buying cocaine or whatever it was I was looking for. Many times they would 'hook me up'. Yes, I did spend a lot of times hanging out in bars. If at one place business was slow, I would go to the next one. Like I said, I was "Jimmy" almost 24 hours a day. Surprisingly, whenever I was off of work and away from my area of responsibility, I did not drink. I just wanted to be me.

I had to maintain the Jimmy character constantly even to those that were not involved in the drug scene. I made it a point to think everyone knew someone that was involved in the drug world. To help keep my sanity, I would take off from work and drive the 600 plus miles to South Texas to be with family and be myself.

•

While attending a meeting with an Assistant US Attorney (AUSA) in Las Cruces regarding one of my federal cases, we (everyone involved with the case) had stayed the night. That same evening, several of us including federal agents decided to eat dinner and visit a club for drinks. Anytime I was in Las Cruces, I felt at ease and could be me instead of having to worry about someone recognize me as Jimmy. We were enjoying the evening and I visited the restroom. As soon as I walked in, I see two people inside a bathroom stall and could hear them snorting something I recognized to be possible cocaine. I went to the sink and taking my time washing my hands. The two guys in the stall came out chatting away. I mentioned something about "that must be some good shit", I was referring to the cocaine. They laughed and said it was. One of them asked if I wanted a hit and I politely turned it down but mentioned something like I would like to buy some for my girl. I was told they were expecting to get some more and would see about getting me some. Inside I felt adrenaline flowing and tried hard to contain my excitement.

I quickly found my boss, who had joined us for our little festivities. I told him about what had just happened and he blew the wind out of my sail, *"Bob, you are not working here, take a break, sit down and drink your beer"*.

•

Another incident that occurred in Las Cruces, again we had gone to a meeting with the Assistant US Attorney (AUSA) on a different federal case I was working on. We decided to go to a local steak house for dinner and drinks. After our meal we went to the bar area and sat at the bar (is this becoming a habit?). The bar was in the shape of a horseshoe. I sat at the end next to the agents that had accompanied me. There were about seven of us and we were trying to wind down after a lengthy meeting. Like I mentioned, I am sitting at the very end when I notice some members of an outlaw motorcycle gang (OMG) from the Las Cruces area walk in.

I am not mentioning names here because of some pending cases. Anyway, this group wearing their rags or colors walked in and sat at the bar across from us. I was trying to make myself unseen by them and trying to think of a way to leave without being noticed by this group. One of the motorcycle gang members happened to notice me and shouted at me, "Jimmy". He motioned for me to sit at the seat next to him and his buddies. Without glancing at my companions, I joined the OMG members on the other side of the bar. My companions who were federal agents picked up on it and knew not to say anything. They appeared to ignored me.

While sitting with the biker member's one of them asked what I was doing in Las Cruces and why I had not called to let them know I was in town. I had previously met them at a biker party in another city. I told them I was passing through heading to Texas and had to stop, eat and relax. We visited for a while and before leaving they asked me to accompany them to another bar. I declined and decided to leave as well. It had been a close call for me.

•

I have had several close calls of being seen by bad guys, talking to police officers. On one particular evening, I was not intentionally working, I had gone to the local casino to relax and listen to the band that happened to be playing on this particular night. The casino at the time, had a second level overlooking the bar and dance floor. I met with a retired police officer and former narcotics agent, standing next to the bar on the ground floor. As I was talking to him, I was interrupted by one of my recent client's body guards. Over the loud music, he pulled me to the side and pointing to the second level, he told me that 'Ramon' wanted to see me. Ramon is the name I will use for this client. I took the elevator to the second level. Ramon was standing at the balcony watching everything going on downstairs in the bar area. Ramon grabbed my arm and pointed to the former officer I had been seen speaking too and in Spanish, he said to me, *"Jimmy, that person you were talking too, stay away from him. He is a Narc". He is a police officer"*. I acted surprised and said, *"Really? I just met him. I am glad you told me"*. During the rest of the evening I remained upstairs with Ramon and his crew.

As an undercover, I tried to make it a habit when out in public, to think and act as if I was Jimmy. I would never know who I would meet. Family members or friends I had in the area, knew not to greet me whenever they would see me in public unless, I greet them first.

•

In my undercover capacity, I got invited to several of my client's parties including to their kids birthday and quincenieras (coming of age) festivities. Some of the bad guy's kids would call me 'Tio Jimmy' (Uncle Jimmy). I would arrive at their home and the kids would run out shouting "Tio Jimmy is here". Deep inside I felt bad for these kids, knowing that one day their parents may be going to prison because of "Tio Jimmy". In retrospect, it is because their parents were selling drugs and the children are the victims.

There were times, I would be in a bad guys house, buying cocaine or methamphetamine and during the transaction, children would be watching the entire deal. A guilt feeling would come to me and I sometimes felt like saying to these kids, "I really am not like this".

•

Once I attended a funeral of a former client (bad guy) who was killed in a car accident while transporting cocaine from another state. Some of cocaine was for me. The funeral was held in a local city and it was decided by my command staff, I should attend and identify any other suspects. I was to gather as much intelligence of the probable suspects. Of course I would be accompanied by a surveillance team and wearing recording devices.

On the day of the funeral, I noticed several people standing in front of the funeral home. I tried to recognize faces so I could walk up and be seen talking to them by those that did not know me. I would walk up to a group of people I had not met, standing around talking to each other. I would offer my condolences and hang out for a bit so those watching me would think I knew the people I was talking too. I then walked over to a next group of people and do the same. I again hang out for a bit, make sure I was seen. I then go into the funeral parlor where family members were sitting, viewing the body and offer my condolence. I know some might think this as being heartless, but a great number of the visitors were known drug suspects and needed to be identified. While inside the funeral parlor, I picked up a brochure that had the names of the pallbearers and other attendees. We did identify other persons in attendance after all.

•

Some of my undercover work was done with the assistance of a confidential informant (CI). Confidential informants were often used for introduction purposes and then they were to be phased out of the case. These CI's would vouch for me, many times telling suspects I was a distant relative or a trustworthy acquaintance.

To have a solid case on an individual, CI's are not to be directly involved in the case to be filed. Confidential Informants are usually persons that are pending charges and have agreed to work for the law enforcement agency for the possibility of having charges on them lowered. I have never seen charges dropped on any of my CI's. Some CI's I had worked with did the work for the money and were not pending charges. I must say, I have worked with some good informants.

●

As an undercover I constantly had to watch my back trail when going home. I would take several routes, constantly watching my rear view mirror for signs of anyone following me. I sure didn't want any of the bad guys knowing where I lived. At times when I had to do personal business, I would unexpectedly meet one of my clients or their associates in a store or out in public. I quickly had to come up with a story because I made it a point to tell them I lived out of town. Some would even ask where I lived to deliver the drugs to my home. I always came up with excuses as to why I didn't want any narcotics coming to my home.

●

I often made myself older than my actual age. My long handlebar mustache was white anyway so it helped me with my story. The reasoning for this, I had hoped the bad guys would not think I was a police officer, thinking I was too old. I did try to keep myself in shape. On my time off, I was always running in the desert. By running in the desert, I was sure not to be seen by anyone and it sure helped in relieving stress. Often times during a run, I would have to go around rattle snakes sunning themselves on a dirt road or path. Somehow, I felt more comfortable around the snakes then most of the bad guys I had to deal with.

●

At the beginning of my undercover work, I was assigned an old white Chevy pickup as my undercover vehicle. In the bed of the truck I carried an old lawn mower and yard tools. I would drive to locations where known crack dealers would actually stand in the streets selling crack cocaine. My security teams were always in tow keeping a close watch on me. I would pull up next to a group of bad guys and a couple of these "fine business men" would walk up to my vehicle and ask what I needed. I would ask for a "50" (fifty dollars' worth) and the dealer would hand me a rock (crack cocaine). I'd give them the money and drive off. In order to have a good solid case, it was necessary to make 3 to 4 purchases from that same individual to prove to a court jury that this same person was indeed distributing crack cocaine or whatever substance they were selling at the time. While doing so, the dealers would notice all the landscaping tools in the back of my vehicle. I was asked by one suspect why I was always buying crack. I told him I had workers helping me in my landscaping business and sometimes I would pay them in crack cocaine. That same person asked if he can come work for me. I told him I would let him know later because work was slow.

During a trial on one of my cases, the defense attorney asked if I had mentioned to his client that I would hire "wet backs" and pay them in crack cocaine. He asked that same question twice emphasizing the word 'Wet Back' to the jury. I answered him by looking directly at the Jury and said, *"No sir, I did not"*. *"I did not say I hire Wet Backs because I do not like that word"*, I continued, *"I told the defendant, I would hire Illegals and pay them in cocaine"*. The presiding District Judge called for a recess an asked us (both attorneys and myself) to his chambers.

The Judge admonished the defense attorney for his use of the word 'Wet Back'. He told me I did a good job of paying attention at the defense attorney's question.

•

For the first two years as an undercover, we never made any arrest of any of the drug suspects that had sold me narcotics. The reason for this was, I didn't have to present myself in court and be identified as to my true identity. While driving around either by myself or with a suspect, I was stopped by the local police for whatever reason. During these stops, I could not identify myself as to my real identity. I would present my UC driver's license with my fake name. Whenever I had an unidentified suspect in my vehicle, the surveillance team would call for a police unit to stop me and identify all the occupants in my vehicle. The officer that made the stop would not know who I really was and gather all of our names and data. It was much later when the police officer would see me in court with a suit and tie, sitting in the waiting room with the rest of the officers. They were surprised to see me.

●

One day I was driving a suspect around town looking for one of his contacts that would sell us crack cocaine. This bad guy kept acting paranoid believing the police were following us. As I was driving, he would direct me to turn at different intersections. At one of the stop signs, my duty weapon happened to slide forward from under my seat. The bad guy saw the gun between my feet and said *"you better hide that before we get stopped by the police"*. I slid the gun back under my seat and said *"Blank the Police"* (add your own explicative here) and kept on driving. I tried to remain calm and remind myself, I was playing the role of a bad guy as well.

●

Being from an older generation of police officer and new to the drug world, I was not familiar with the present street language or terminology. A bad guy and I were riding around looking for one of his contacts so I could purchase crack cocaine. The surveillance team was following us at a distance. The bad guy sitting in the passenger seat kept glancing at the passenger door side mirror and turning around to look behind us. All of a sudden, the suspect tells me to " *flip a bitch*". Now I have never heard that terminology so I am looking for someone to flip off. I keep driving straight and again he said "flip a bitch". I asked him what he meant by that and he said make a "U-turn". So I make a U-turn in the middle of the block. Meanwhile I am thinking to myself, Had I of done this on my off time, I probably would have been stopped by the police and cited. Many times while driving with bad guys, I would in some way break a traffic law and not get stopped by the law.

●

As I got comfortable working as an undercover, making small purchases, I soon began purchasing larger quantity of drugs, either cocaine or methamphetamine; sometimes both at the same time. While making purchases of either type of narcotics, I was involved with two different classes of people. I am not racially nor ethnically profiling here. It's just the way it was in the streets. When purchasing cocaine, I was involved more with the Mexican culture as most of the cocaine was being smuggled in from Mexico by Mexican nationals. A lot of the suspects I dealt with had ties to the Cartels, forcing me to change my personality and act in accordance when dealing with these types of people. I knew, I always had back up but they were seconds or minuets away and had to survive until help arrived. I would play the role in ways that suited me and the bad guys.

My involvement with methamphetamine (meth) dealers or traffickers causes me to act differently. Meth affects users differently than cocaine. Most users of meth are addicted in a much harsher manner, affecting the body, teeth and mind. The small time dealers, the ones who sold meth by the gram were the ones that worried me the most. They always seemed to be high and would do anything to rip you off. Traffickers who sold by the ounce, pound or kilo were less likely to rip you off. Most were in business not for themselves but for someone else and owed money to the supplier. They wanted to keep you as a client because they were sure they were going to get paid.

I have made numerous purchases of both different product and learned to change the way I played my role among these two kinds of dealers. Strangely, I was more comfortable around the cocaine dealers than the methamphetamine dealers. I never lost perspective and knew that any of these people could be just as dangerous at any given time.

Mexican Cartel began to develop methamphetamine in large quantities. It was my understanding; it was easier to obtain the right ingredients to make the product in Mexico. I never got myself involved in the production side. I just knew that locally made or homemade meth was dangerous to produce as it is known to be highly volatile. Much of the homemade version was made in local residence or the back of pickups. The small time dealers were using their own product and causing them to waste their life away. These were the least I liked having any involvement with.

•

Prior to beginning an operation, everyone involved in the operation would brief and go over an operational plan including the signals I would give if I got into trouble. Since most of the time on an operation I would wear a cowboy hat, the signal I gave, was for me to throw my hat on the ground if I got in trouble. If any of the team saw me throwing my hat on the ground, they knew I was in trouble and respond immediately to assist. Thankfully I never had to do that. Whenever I had an audio monitor on me, I would say a certain code word or phrase for whenever I got into trouble. As I have mentioned, in every operation, I had surveillance tailing me. It was always in the back of my mind, worrying, what if the audio transmitter was not working. It has happened before.

The times when I would be out in public, if I went into a bar at night, I', make it a habit to call one of the agents and let them know where I was in case I needed help or found a contact that wanted to sell me some type of narcotic. I would never make any purchases narcotics on my own, or without being monitored. This was not only for my safety but for the integrity of the case. In most cases the task force provided me with operational funds to purchase dinner or drinks to potential clients. It was allowed as long as it was documented on how the money was spent. I have been asked if I kept receipts. Only cops or bean counters asked for receipts and it was not a good idea for me to ask for a receipt in front of bad guys.

I always played the part of a buyer, a person of affluence; I had money if I was a buyer of large amounts of cocaine and/or methamphetamine. Keep in mind; most of the bad guys selling larger amounts were in it for the money. If they saw me throwing money around, their focus would be on that. Police on duty did not spend money; much less buy drinks for someone else.

Some operations I worked on, another agent would play the part of my body guard. It served several purposes. One, it was extra eyes to witness transactions and two, my safety. A great majority of my cases were done without a second undercover agent. Often times I felt like I preferred to not have assistance because, I not only had to worry about myself but the safety of the agent in that particular case.

I did however have an excellent female partner/agent that worked very well in many of my cases (I will call her Kat). Kat made the perfect partner, she was always observant and could remember license plates and details. Being much younger than I, often times she played the part of my niece. I would take her on lot of cases with me and everyone in the bad guy world knew her as "my niece". We worked a case in a certain store talking to the owners who are our suspects and Kat would say to me "*Tio Jimmy can you buy me this*", pointing to a certain item. She played the perfect part. One day the suspect's wife was in the store when Kat and I walked in. The suspect's wife and Kat were discussing a shopping trip to Lubbock. Kat asked me in front of her to give her a credit card to go shopping. She knew I didn't have any such card but Hey, I was the rich uncle.

Kat and I in our undercover capacity were invited to a ranch where the bad guys had race horses. While there, someone would saddle up a horse just so Kat could ride. They really liked her. With her at my side, again it was for safety reason and by having a female along, it would help put the suspects at ease.

Kat had her ways with practical jokes on me as well. Kat and I were meeting with a suspect outside his feed store and we were standing next to a trailer loaded with hay. On the trailer was a rope about 5 feet long with a snap hook on the end. As I was talking to the suspect, unknowingly Kat hooked the snap hook to my back belt loop. At the end of the conversation Kat and I were walking towards my vehicle until I reached the end of the rope. It jerked me back so hard I almost fell. She thought that was funny.

I had my jokingly ways with Kat as well; once while driving down the highway; I saw buzzards on the highway. I mentioned to her, I would like to catch one and keep it as a pet. She said that would be cool. I asked if she would help me catch one and she asked, how? I told her she can lie down on the side of the highway and pretend she was a dead carcass and when the buzzards got near her she could reach and grab its legs and hold it. I would then rush over to help her. She didn't think that was a good plan.

●

Kat and I were working an undercover buy in another city. We wound up in our target suspect's trailer house buying cocaine. The suspect (a Cuban) had invited us in and we stood in the living room where we could watch the suspect and the front door. The suspect had a friend who came in after we did and stood in front of the door to watch us and the transaction. Our surveillance team were a few blocks away. The purchase was made without a hitch and we left. It was during our debriefing at the office where I found out Kat and I were thinking the same thing. If anything was to go wrong during the buy, we were both going to rush the guy standing blocking the doorway. Both of us were thinking on hitting him hard pushing him through the glass door. Thank God it went well.

●

The particular suspect mentioned above, we met him on an operation arranged by another local task force. We had heard that a certain band was playing that evening and some of the band members were suspected cocaine traffickers. With the assistance of another UC, it was planned that Kat and I were to go in as a couple and the other UC would play the part of our body guard (I will call him BG). BG looked the part with his long goat tee, tattoos all over his arms. As we walked in, I was recognized in my undercover capacity by the owner of the club and he gave us VIP tags and sat us in the very front next to the dance floor. The local task force provided us with funds or spending money. From where we were sitting, some of the patrons had recognized me (Jimmy) they would walk up to greet me. The UC playing the part of my body guard (BG) would get up from his seat, stop them and ask what they wanted. They would respond, they wanted to say hello to Jimmy. I motion to BG to let them through. These people would greet me and Kat and pay their respect as it is done in the Mexican culture.

Meanwhile, we had a team of surveillance agents inside the club looking for potential customers. Upon identifying a potential client they would send me or Kat a text message with the description of the suspect. My job was to attempt to meet them and make a purchase. I received a text message from one of the surveillance agents saying *"the black guy dressed in all white is your target"*. After reading the text, I showed to the message to Kat and BG. I told BG to send a round of drinks to the people at the table behind us and I would return shortly.

I stood up, looked around until I spotted the suspect mentioned in the text message. He was standing near the entrance to the restrooms. I walked up to him and stuck out my hand to shake his and said, *"Hey remember me from Hobbs"*. Initially the Cuban said he did and shook my hand. I left it at that and went into the restroom. After leaving the restroom, I went back to the Cuban and stood next to him as if I was enjoying the music. I turned to him and said *"hey can you sell me the same thing you did in Hobbs?"* The suspect looked at me and said *"you must have me confused with someone else because I don't know you"*. I apologized and started to walk away. The Cuban came after me stopped me and asked what I needed. I told him, I was sorry and I had him confused with someone in Hobbs that had sold me some powder (cocaine). He asked how much I needed and told him I wanted to buy a gram for my girl. He asked where I was parked, I told him around the building. The Cuban told me to follow him and we went outside of the club. I knew I was being watched by the surveillance team stationed outside the club. I followed the suspect out to the parking lot. He asked where I was parked and I pointed to my undercover vehicle park at the side of building.

I got into the driver's side and the Cuban climbed into the passenger side of the vehicle. He reached into his pocket and pulled out a baggie containing several individual baggies with cocaine in each of them. I asked him for the price and he said to give him a hundred dollars. Since I had given all the money to BG, I had about $97.00 in change and told him that is all I had on me now. He took it. I told him I was looking for a reliable contact where I can buy larger quantities of cocaine. I asked him for his number because I needed someone I can trust and I too had clients relying on me to sell cocaine to them. The Cuban provided me with his number and the assurance of him being reliable. We both got out of my UC vehicle and went back inside the club. With my chest pounding with excitement because I had scored, I got to where my partners were seated; I sat next to Kat and BG. Kat asked where I had gone and with a big grin, I pulled out the little baggie of cocaine from my shirt pocket. My heart was beating almost out of my throat with excitement.

Once the cocaine was in my possession, I knew we had to leave the club. As per policy we had to put the freshly acquired cocaine in the evidence vault at the task force. We held a de-briefing of what had just transpired in the club. This is one of my favorite nights. Purchases such as these are known as 'cold buys' because an informant was not used to initiate the transaction therefore making it a better case. During my career I have made many cold buys. Each time I experience the same adrenaline rush.

•

On slower days I would hang out at the local casino. Anyone of the agents doing surveillance, who recognized a known trafficker sitting at one of the slot machines, would text me of the potential suspect's location. At this particular time, I was accompanied by a second agent who played the part of my employee and body guard. We located I had been referred too, and I sat at the machine next to them. The second agent, stood behind me acting as my bodyguard and handing me money as I needed. Sitting next to the suspect, I'd begin casual conversation by asking how a certain slot machine worked because I was new to this. This particular lady I met at the slot machines explained how the slots worked. I recalled saying to her in casual conversation I was waiting for my supplier to bring my cocaine but he never showed. She acted as if she didn't hear me and finally asked how much I was waiting for. I told her a couple of grams. She said she could probably help me out but she would have to go to the bathrooms and would be right back. The lady got up from her seat and walked towards the restrooms. After returning to her seat at the slots, she carefully handed me to little plastic bindles of cocaine. I motioned for my partner to give her the money. My partner paid for the cocaine and I asked if I could perhaps get more from her since I wanted to find someone locally who I can rely on. She assured me I can rely on her and gave me her phone number. We eventually ended up making several large purchases from this lady, I just happened to meet at the casino.

•

The casino was one of my favorite places to conduct my business. During horse racing season, I would hang out at the casino or at the stables where many of the trainers or groomers were located. I made several narcotics cases at either of the locations. The casino was also the location of my arrests or take downs. Upon completion of a case, it was decided by the bosses or case agents to initiate the take downs (arrests) at the casino parking lot. The casino had excellent cameras both inside and outside. They were always monitoring and recording. It was the perfect location for the surveillance teams to blend in among the parked cars and casino's patrons. During the take downs, I would be arrested alongside the suspects. We tried to always make the arrest out in the parking lot of the casino to keep the public safe in the event that something went wrong. The arrest teams would force us all on the ground and place handcuffs on us. I was treated the same as the suspects being arrested. I knew better than try to resist for fear of being tased to make everything look authentic. I am not a fan of electricity and therefore did not want to be tased. Once the suspects are whisked away, I am driven across the street and the handcuffs removed. On several occasions I would be face down on the parking lot with my hands cuffed behind my back, I recalled seeing the casino's patrons walk by and look at us. I wonder what they must have been thinking.

On several occasions when the suspects were interviewed by the arresting agents, I, in my undercover capacity, was named by the suspect as the one selling the drugs. There is no honor among us crooks.

•

A great number of these traffickers are not too bright. I was in a suspect's house buying methamphetamine when he asked if I was the Police, as he handed me the little bindle of meth I just purchased. I actually told him and I do not know why I said it; I was with the drug task force. The bad guy laughed it off and still handed me the meth. I guess he thought I was joking. Too bad for him.

Another example, I went to this crack dealer's house to make my third purchase from this same individual. As I get to the front door I am met buy a younger male bad guy who asked me what I needed. I told him I was looking for Davis (not his real name). This person told me his uncle is not home. Needing to make the third buy from my suspect, I told this individual, I would return at a later time. The individual asked me what I needed and I told him I was looking for some rock but I would return later. Again he asked what I needed. I told him I didn't know him and would rather do business with Davis. I was actually hoping he would sell to me because it would be a new contact for me. The suspect pulled out his wallet and removed a driver's license. He handed it to me saying "I'm so and so (again not real name), Davis is my uncle, I can hook you up". "Wow! Got me another one", I thought to myself. Acting reluctantly, I said ok. He went inside for a few minutes and returned with the crack cocaine. I guess that is why they call it DOPE.

•

While in an undercover capacity, no one views you as a police officer (at least they had better not) if you are doing your job correctly, you are just another trafficker, junkie or tweaker. Anything is bound to happen around you. Things happen in front of police officers while they are on duty and in uniform, therefore, things are bound to happen in front of you while working undercover.

On one particular operation, I was at a suspect's residence about to make a methamphetamine buy. I had previously made a couple of purchases from the female suspect on prior occasions. I placed my order and she to the next house over to get the meth from her source. I returned to my vehicle to wait for her to return. The suspect had been gone a few minutes and while watching my side mirror, I noticed a red pickup truck park in the street directly behind me. The driver was a black male and I saw a white male and his wife or girlfriend get out of the pickup. I could hear they were arguing with the black driver. The female ran up to the house where my female suspect had entered. I saw the driver of the pickup exit his vehicle. The white male's wife or girlfriend came out of the house holding a rifle. She handed the rifle to the white male who at this time was being chased around the pickup by the black driver. I was thinking to myself this is going to get good. I also had hoped the surveillance team could see what was going on. I saw the black driver wrestle the rife from the white male and the rifle went off during the struggle. By the sound of it, it sounded like a 22 caliber. The black male, took the rifle away from the white male and hit him on the head with the stock of the rifle, breaking the rifle in two. I had my cell phone below the door window level where it could not be seen from the outside and contacted the surveillance team. I wanted to let them know what was going on. I one of my surveillance team members to contact the police department and report what was going on. The fight stopped as quickly as it began. The driver of the pickup got into the truck and drove off. The male and female involved picked up the pieces of the rifle and went into their house. I did notice the female limping. I later found out she had been shot in the ass when the rifle went off during the struggle.

The female suspect, I had been waiting for, returned with the meth. I had been standing at the curb, in front of the suspect's residence when the police units arrived. I did not know if they (police) recognized me, but I told them *"there was nothing to see here, everything was fine"*. As soon as the patrol vehicle's left the female suspect handed me the meth.

●

As mentioned before, in this line of work, I found that there is a huge difference between working with crack cocaine/cocaine dealers and methamphetamine dealers. Those that sell in large amounts such as pounds and/or kilos acted differently. I say different in the way that business is conducted.

Many or most of the larger scale traffickers have ties to the cartels in Mexico and I have met and done business with a few. These type of operations are long and tiresome. Tiresome, especially for the surveillance teams that put in tons of boring hours following me around, watching me act like I may be enjoying myself (Ok, I may have been enjoying myself a little). The surveillance team agents would spend hours in their vehicles keeping an eye on me from afar or listening to my conversation with the bad guys over the audio transmitters I had on my person.

One of the main objectives of a narcotics task force is; identify and dismantle Drug Trafficking Organization (DTOs). Often it is accomplished at a local level by making purchases beginning with lower level dealers and moving up the ladder to a main supplier.

In all cases involving the sales of illegal narcotics, everyone has a supplier, beginning with the street level dealer to the main supplier. It is our focus to get to the main supplier or as high up the ladder as we can. These DTO's have a chain of command as well. Much of the higher up dealers are south of the border. I have met and purchased narcotics from bad guys with ties to the Juarez, Carrillo-Fuentes and La Familia Cartels. As we all know are in Mexico. I have been asked on several occasions if any of the Cartels are here in the United States. Yes they are and they have always been here. If any drugs are coming into the US, someone on this side of the border is involved and is closely tied o the Mexican cartel. The Mexican drug organizations have risen extensively since the demise of the Columbian cartels. The larger cities in the US seem to be the hubs of these DTO's. The major drugs coming into the country go to the larger cities and from there it is distributed to the surrounding cities. Like I always have said, drugs come north and the money always goes south. I could write more about the cartels and DTO's but it would take another entire book. I will leave it as is for now.

•

On several occasion I would be invited to a Bar-B-Que or a party at some bad guy's house during the hot summer months and the surveillance team would have to sit in their vehicles far enough away cursing me. I say cursing because I actually received text messages from the agents with threats from the team to "hurry the blank up". Meanwhile I am suffering as well, having to drink cold beers with the bad guys. Anyway, it always was good to know that if I ever got in trouble, the team would be there. I have the greatest respect for all my former team members.

Whenever I could, I would carry more than one recording or transmitter devise because Private Murphy of Murphy's Law fame (remember him?), followed me from the Marine Corps and somethings always went wrong when it came to manmade electronic devices. Audio and/or video devises were always good to have during an operation. When the case would go to trial, suspects have testified in court, it was not them, they didn't sell me anything or it was entrapment. During the trial, the DA would play the video or audio to the Jury and guess what? Bye Bye. In most cases, when the defense receives copies of the case recording, the defense would make a motion to forgo the trial and ask for a plea bargain.

•

Regarding recording devises, on one particular operation in another city, I was to meet with a known trafficker and make arrangements to purchase 4-6 ounces of methamphetamine. We met in a local sports bar and grill. I was wearing an ink pen that was also a video recorder. On the backside of the pen, there was a little blue light that would illuminate anytime the video recorder was activated. When on operations, I made it a habit to place a piece of black tape to cover the light. During the meet with the suspect inside the sports bar, I noticed he kept looking down at my shirt pocket where I had the ink pen. The suspect was wearing sun glasses inside the sports bar and removed them. He pointed at my ink pen and asked why there is a blue light coming from my pen. Right away, I knew what he was referring too. My first thought was, I forgot to cover up the blue light with the black tape. I told the bad guy it must be the reflection of the lights inside the bar. The bar had Christmas lights strung above it. My brain housing group was working over time trying to figure a way out of this. To my good fortune, I received a text message from someone not involved in the case and quickly told the suspect, I was getting a phone call and needed to take it out side. I told him it was business.

I stood up and acted like I was speaking to someone on the phone. I walked directly out the front door trying not to panic. With my back towards the front door of the bar, I pressed on the top button of the ink pen/video recorder to turn it off. Anyway I thought I did. While outside I contacted the case agent, a Special Agent (SA) in charge of the operation and told him what happened. He thought for a moment and advised maybe I should call off the meet and leave the area. I told him I could salvage it and to let me handle it. He asked if I felt comfortable with the case based on what just occurred. I told him I would continue with the meeting. The case agent agreed and allowed me to continue. Thinking I had turned off the video recorder, I went back in the bar (again gentile readers, Pvt. Murphy accompanied me here).

Once back inside to continue the meet, I told the bad guy some BS story about some of my employees giving me a hard time. I was sitting there with the suspect and again he removed his sun glasses and pointed to my ink pen. I glanced down at the pen and I could see the blue light behind the pen, reflecting on my shirt. I am really trying to remain calm by this time. The bad guy became suspicious once again and asked where I had gotten the pen. I told him it was a gift from someone. I took the pen out of my pocket, removed the cap and scribbled on a napkin. I replaced the pen back into my pocket. He again mentioned the blue light. I told him it's the reflection of the bar lights and quickly changed the subject. He left it at that, but I could tell he was very suspicious and nervous. The suspect reluctantly agreed to meet later that evening with 6 ounces methamphetamine.

After checking my back trail to make sure I had not been followed, I met with the case agent and surveillance team, in the federal building for a debriefing. It was highly recommended by several parties involved that my case had been compromised and I should call it off. The SA in charge of this operation, asked how I felt about it. I told him, I still felt I could save the case and if allowed, I would continue with the meet and purchase of the methamphetamine. The SA agreed and said we would give it a shot if I really felt comfortable.

The bad guy and I agreed to meet at a local department store, parking lot, later that evening to make the deal. When time came for the purchase, I drove to the department store parking lot where I contacted the bad guy on his cell phone. The bad guy said he would be on his way. The time came for the bad guy to arrive however he never arrived. I waited longer and tried to call him several times. Meanwhile I kept in contact with the case agent by phone as well. The bad guy was not answering my phone calls. By this time the agents on the surveillance teams began questioning if the suspect was 'hinked' (suspicious about me) up and if he would show. I received calls from the team members to call off the deal as they did not feel comfortable about this and feared for my safety. Shortly after, I got the call from the bad guy saying he was on his way but wanted to move the meeting location to a different place. I will add, buy this time my nerves were almost shot. I called the SA (case agent) to advise him about the change of location. Since it was getting dark and too many wrong things had happened, it causes me to think twice about the deal. The SA advised me it may be a good idea on calling the operation off as too many red flags had been raised. The SA instructed all involved to meet in the parking area of an undisclosed area,

Prior to me leaving the department store's parking lot, I called the bad guy and made up the story the deal was off because there were too many police cars in the area and I felt like I was being followed by narcotic agents in undercover vehicles. I told him I would call him later and hung up.

All the agents were waiting on me as I arrived. I got out of my vehicle and returned the buy money to the SA. We were all standing around the parking lot, discussing the event, when I saw the bad guy's vehicle driving slowly around the block. I was sure he had seen us. We decided to call it quits for the night and regroup early the next day.

Once I climb in my undercover vehicle, I called the suspect and made up the story, I was followed by narcs and had been pulled over by them. I said this in case he had seen me in the parking lot. He later confirmed he had seen me talking to some people. I went on by telling him, they had stopped me and wanted to seize the money I had to buy the methamphetamine. I told the suspect the agents didn't seize the money because I had showed them a receipt I had for selling some roping horses. I guess he bought that story because I did wind up buying a total of 9 ounces from him at a later time.

In an undercover operation, it's everyone involved in the case, responsibility to look for warning signs. If something did not look or feel right, it should be addressed. If someone felt it was not safe to continue the operation then they would recommend calling off the operation. The final word goes to the undercover and the case agent.

•

As a police officer, I was known for my internal pranks; however, I was not immune to pranks being done to me, especially with in the narcotics unit. Narcs can be the worst if you ask me.

During one operation, it was planned, I was to "order up" (make the call and order the drugs) a certain amount of narcotics and meet with the suspect. After I make the purchase, the surveillance team would rush in and arrest the suspect. Since this case was going federal, we had Federal Special Agents with us as well from a certain alphabet agency. The call was made and I told the suspect I would pick him up so we can make the deal. We chose a location away from the public to initiate the take down (arrest). I went to the suspect's house, picked him up and drove to the predetermined location.

While at the location, the suspect and I were standing outside my undercover truck and I received a text message from this certain Special Agent's cell phone saying something about how good I looked out there and my Wranglers looked good on me. I read the text and laughed, thinking nothing of it. The take down occurred and the suspect was arrested. One of our agents was interviewing the suspect at the scene. I received another text from SA phone and again it got kind of personal. I recalled thinking, this cannot be coming from SA. He was a federal agent and a no nonsense kind of agent. I received another text from SA's phone and I got worried.

I played it in my mind, I knew and worked with this SA this past summer in another city. It cannot be coming from him since I knew he was married and could not be gay. I was thinking to myself that if it continued, how would I approached his supervisor with this complaint. Anyway, the operation was over and I decided to keep this to myself for the time being (don't get ahead of me readers).

The following morning, we were in morning briefing at the task force office and the task force deputy commander asked me what was up between me and SA? I asked what he meant by that. He continued by saying that during yesterday's operation, SA kept giving me complements while they both were sitting in the car watching me.

I immediately, let loose and showed the deputy commander the texts I received from SA's phone and said I was worried about this. Everyone began laughing and one of the agents told me that SA had left his phone unsecured and the deputy commander got it and began sending me those text messages. Later on, SA came to the task force for a briefing and we told him what had happened. We all got a laugh out of that one. SA has since moved to a larger city and every now and then I will receive a text from him saying how good I look in my jeans.

•

There was an operation I was involved with where my quick tongue and experience came into play.

I was temporarily assigned to different task force. I was to meet with a suspect and deliver money, $12,000, to a confidential informant who was working another case. My job was to go to the task force hand the money to the case agent and in turn, he would give it to an informant to pay the bad guy that had driven in from Phoenix. Once there I was advised I was to play the part of the buyer and money man. The informant and the dealer from Phoenix were going to a local restaurant for lunch. My part in this was to go to the restaurant, sit at a different table and the informant would introduce me as the buyer/money man.

When the time came, I entered the restaurant and sat at a table near the front entrance. It was far enough away from the informant and the trafficker/bad guy but I could keep them in sight. I was seated near the cash registered. The informant and his guest finished their lunch and went to the register to pay. Out of the corner of my eyes I could see the informant point towards my direction, saying something to the suspect and a lady they were with. They glanced at me and the male bad guy smiled and nodded towards me. I nodded my head in return. I was later informed by the informant; he had told the suspect I was the money man and his boss.

Later that week, I was again assigned to the task force to be the undercover for the case. The bad guy's cell number was provided to me. I was told to call the number and tell the bad guy that my employee (informant) was in jail and I was to take over the purchases because he was using my money. I told the bad guy I still wanted my pound of methamphetamine. The suspect agreed to drive down to New Mexico from Phoenix with my meth and I was to give him $11,000, money that was owed on a previous buy from the informant.

To not confuse anyone, the $11,000 was a partial payment of money that was previously owed to the bad guy. During this operation, a lot of dope was fronted and partial payments were made. This kept us owing the bad guy money. In the real world, if money was not paid up, someone was getting hurt, meaning 'Moi'.

The date was set when the suspect agreed to drive to my location and bring me the pound of methamphetamine. Several federal, state and local agents were on hand to provide surveillance and back up. The plan was for me in my undercover capacity, to officially meet the bad guy at the casino and complete the deal. The local casino again was the ideal location because of its surveillance cameras inside and out in the parking lot. At the time, there was only one main entrance to the parking lot and it could easily be covered by surveillance.

The time came for the suspect to arrive and every one of our agents were in place. The bad guy called me on my cell phone and asked me to meet with him outside and to look for a blue jeep. I went outside, spotted the

Jeep and met with my new found friend. The bad guy told me he was not comfortable in doing any business at our present location, mentioning the casino's cameras. He asked if I knew of a better location. He went on to say he had the meth in a hidden compartment in his jeep and wanted a safe place to remove it. I told him I did know of a place and asked him to follow me. I got into my undercover vehicle and drove to the new location. During the drive, I contacted the surveillance team to let them know about the change of location.

I drove to a secluded location next to the local drag strip. The supplier parked his vehicle next to my vehicle. He was accompanied by the lady I had seen him with when they were at the restaurant. They both got out of the Jeep. The bad guy went to the rear of the jeep and removed the rear tail light. I saw him reach into a hollow place behind the removed tail light. He pulled out a clear plastic sealed bag that contained the methamphetamine. He then handed me the bag of meth and I inspected it. I reached into my vehicle and handed the supplier a paper bag with the $11,000 dollars that had been supplied to me from the task force. The suspect reached back into the hollow compartment and pulled out two more one pound bags of methamphetamine. He told me he had to deliver that to someone else but could not get in contact with him. I told him to let me have the meth and he can tell the person this was meant for to call me. The bad guy handed me the two extra pounds of meth. I recall my heart was about to explode with excitement. This is the first time we had actually met and here he is fronting me a kilo of methamphetamine. Before replacing the tail light, the bad guy removed a couple of hundred dollars bills from the money I had given him and he placed the rest in the hollow compartment in the jeep.

After the bad guy and the girl left, I was trying to control my excitement, I called the commander of the task force and told him the transaction was complete and was in route to the task force. As soon as I entered the task force office with a big grin, I showed the agents the plastic bag containing one pound and then pulled out two more pounds of meth saying "*he gave me this*". Everyone seemed to be excited upon seeing the unexpected extra pounds of methamphetamine.

A week later, I was called by the commander of the task force and asked to call the same supplier in my undercover capacity. I was to set up another purchase. I called the bad guy in Phoenix and told him I had more money for him and I needed more meth to be brought down to my location. The plan was to take the supplier down on this next meet. On the day of the deal, I called the bad guy and asked if everything was still going to happen as planned. He told me, everything was good and he had sent the girl he was with the last time, with the meth and she would pick up the money I supposedly had for him. I believe I owed him around sixty thousand dollars. I relayed the conversation to the Special Agent (SA) in charge of the case. I was told that they needed the supplier down here as well so he could be arrested. I told them I would come up with something.

I placed a call to the bad guy and told him, I was not comfortable dealing with any women and I needed him to bring me the meth or I would call the whole thing off. I told him I have been in this business for so long without being caught. I added I like to do things my way and my way was the safe way. The bad guy asked me to give him a moment and he would call me back. After a few minutes he returned my call and said he had contacted the girl and told her to return to Phoenix. The supplier said he would be on his way with the product and he would collect the money I supposedly owed him. I relayed the information to the SA and the excitement began to fill the room.

Later that evening, the supplier called and said he was almost to my location. I had previously told him we would again meet at the casino. When the time arrived to meet at the casino, everyone was in place to initiate the take down and arrest. The plan was for me to be arrested as well. The bad guy contacted me and said he was in the parking lot of the casino. I told him, I was inside the casino and to join me inside. I wanted time enough to ensure everyone involved in the arrest would be in place for the take down. I was a bit nervous because I was supposed to hand him over $64,000 I did not have. In the drug world, this is the occasion where people get hurt or worst. So yes, I was nervous.

The met me in the casino and a short time later we walked out towards my vehicle. I told him that I would go to my vehicle and get the money and he can go get the packages (meth). I remember intentionally walking slowly to my truck looking around for the arrest team. The bad guy was walking towards my vehicle and I intentionally fumbled with my keys giving time for the arrest team to arrive. All kinds of scenarios were running wild in my head. I was trying to stall as much as possible to give time for the arrest team. I distinctly recall thinking "it was taking a long time for the arrest team", "maybe they hadn't seen me", what if my audio devises were not working and they couldn't hear what was happening". All kinds of thoughts were going through my head. It may have been seconds but at the time those seconds were dragging. I definitely did not want to get to my vehicle and not have the money, which could escalate this deal into bigger problems.

It then happened in a flash. Unmarked police vehicles quickly surrounded us, and agents came rushing in with guns drawn yelling "get on the ground". I too was placed on the ground along with the suspect and the woman that was with him. As we lay on the asphalt of the parking lot, we were handcuffed and told to shut up and not move. While on the ground, I could see casino patrons walking around us. I noticed a New Mexico State Police unit blocking the main entrance to the casino as there was a second vehicle involved and had attempted to get away. The driver of that vehicle didn't get too far and turned out to be a relative of the supplier.

After all the bad guys were secured and taken away, I was placed in an unmarked police car as well and driven across the street where my handcuffs were removed. As I was on the ground, I could hear my partner Kat who was part of the arrest team, saying something about 'tasing' me. Meaning she wanted someone to use the Taser on me knowing I did not like electricity.

Operation Crystal Palace

We had received intelligence of a rather large operation involving large amounts of methamphetamine being distributed in the southwest region of the United States. I was once again detailed to work as the undercover (UC) on this case. The task force initiating the case needed an undercover to infiltrate this drug trafficking organization that had ties to a drug cartel in Mexico. I had the occasion in meeting Beto (not his real name) a known local methamphetamine trafficker. I mentioned to Beto, I would buy methamphetamine in small amounts at first and if all went well I could move up to purchasing larger quantities. At the initial introduction, I met Beto's father a known trafficker as well. Beto later mentioned me his father had told him not to make any deals with me because he was told I may be a police officer. Beto went on to say, he did not believe it and I did not look like a cop. He said he would "hook me up" meaning he would get the meth I wanted. Beto asked me to not mention anything to his father about our agreement.

I had made a couple of smaller purchases of meth of around 3 to 6 ounces. On one occasion, I told Beto I wanted to buy a pound of meth because I had clients out of state who wanted meth. Beto said he knew someone who could get it for me. Beto made a call to a person he claimed to be his uncle. Beto told the uncle, who I will call Elias; I wanted to purchase a pound of meth and could pay for it. I was given an address and told to go to the uncle's residence and he would call his uncle to meet me outside.

I drove to the address provided to me by Beto with my surveillance team in tow. After I arrived, I parked in front of the small framed house. I called Beto on his cell phone and told him to call his uncle and tell him I was outside. Shortly Elias came out and walked to the passenger side of my vehicle. He opened the door and while standing between the door and cab of my vehicle, he pulled out a cellophane wrapped package from inside of his shirt. He handed me the package. I examined the package and when I was satisfied it was methamphetamine, I gave Elias a paper sack containing $19,000.00 as previously agreed. Elias didn't bother to look in the bag. He just asked how much was in there and I told him. I then asked if I could call him directly the next time I need to purchase more. Elias said it was alright and provided me with his number. I left ad returned to the task force with the meth.

On the next purchase, the planned was, I would meet with Elias's supplier who would be driving down from Phoenix. The "buy walk" (a term used when buying narcotics and no arrest made) was to take place in a different city. Arrangements were made to rent two hotel rooms side by side. I would occupy one room with surveillance equipment in place. The room next door would be occupied by the backup/surveillance team. The team could monitor the transaction via video and audio. Again, I emphasize more than one audio/video was used.

Inside the room, I occupied, I placed a chair in the corner next to the bed. I put the money I was using for the purchase under the mattress, along with my trusty Sig Sauer 40 caliber firearm. I had purposely placed the chair in the corner so if I sat down during the transaction, I wanted my back to the wall and my weapon handy. In case something went wrong during this transaction and the surveillance team had to rush in, I wanted to be out of the line of fire. The team had an extra key card to the room I was in.

The initial plan was for me to allow Elias and the supplier into the room. However, as usual, most plans change at any given time. While in the room, I received a call from Elias informing me, he and the supplier were out in the parking lot. He wanted me to meet them outside. I told him I would not because; there was too much traffic outside, both vehicle and pedestrian and I didn't want to raise any suspicion. I told Elias I would meet with them at the side door and I would let them in. As I opened the side door, I noticed Elias with two other unknown Hispanic males with him. I opened the side door and was greeted by Elias. Elias then introduced me to a younger looking Hispanic he called Jose. I let them in and the third male wearing a large un-tucked t-shirt, followed in behind them. On the last person that walked in, I noticed the outline of what looked like a weapon in the small of his back under the shirt. My brain housing group was working overtime thinking of a contingency plan now that a third person was involved. I thought about insisting he stay outside but then I thought, "*hey what the hell, the more the merrier and it's another subject we can ID and arrest*". I escorted the group to my room, purposely making extra noise to alert the surveillance team we were about to enter the room. After opening the door to my room, I allowed them to enter first. Intentionally I left the room's door, deadbolt lock unlocked in case the surveillance team needed to bust in.

Once introductions were made again, I noticed the third subject was not introduced. I concluded he was acting as security for the other two. As I began making small talk, I eased myself to the corner of the room to be near my weapon. I asked Jose if he brought the package, referring to the meth and he said he had it in his car. The third, unidentified bad guy purposely stretched allowing me to see an automatic weapon in the front waist band of his jeans. I surmised he wanted to show me he was armed. I got kind of worried because I didn't know if it was the same gun he had in the small of his back and I did not see him move it to the front or perhaps he was carrying two guns.

Elias asked if I had the money, I lifted the mattress to allow him to see the bag I had the money in and to purposely see I had a weapon as well. I told Jose to go get the package. Jose told me he had it in a compartment under the car and he would need to jack up the car to remove it from a hidden compartment. He went on to say he had to take the car to a secluded place so he can remove the package. I told him I had time to wait and he could go and do what he needed to do. Leaving the third unknown bad guy behind, Jose and Elias left the room.

The third bad guy who had remained in the room with me was too quiet and seems a bit uptight. I offered him a beer I already had in the room to help calm nerves. He gladly accepted. After approximately an hour, I heard a knock on the door. It was Elias and Jose. They had returned.

Once back in the room, Jose reached into the front of his pants and removed a cellophane wrapped package similar to the last pound of meth I had purchased. He handed me the methamphetamine and I examined it. After I was satisfied it was probably meth, I handed the bag containing the nineteen grand to Jose. I say probably meth because in reality the only sure way to test it is either to use it or test it with an approved chemical kit.

Jose took the bag with the money, sat at the round table in the room and began counting the money. He counted out all nineteen grand. He then gave Elias and the third subject some money. We talked a little longer and before they left, we agreed to continue to do more business in the near future. I breathed a big sigh of relief once my adrenaline began to subside.

The individuals involved in this case were all subsequently arrested as a result of a very well laid plan. The arrest phase involved several federal, state, county and local police agencies. During the arrest, several pounds of methamphetamine were seized as well as firearms. Incidentally, a loaded Uzi automatic was found behind the driver's seat of Elias's vehicle. Elias's small children were in the vehicle as well. Elias and his family planned to leave the state with the money they were supposed to get from me.

To ensure a safe operation, many hours of planning, surveillance and time away from family was provided by all agents involved.

Operation Los Amigos

Operations Los Amigos was first initiated at the local level that quickly evolved to a connection of a major drug trafficking organization. It all began with introduction by a confidential informant to a target that had been on the radar for a while. I was introduced to an individual I will call Sammy. Sammy had been distributing cocaine in southeast New Mexico and west Texas for a while. The introduction was made at a local casino. At this first meeting, I purchased a couple of ounces of cocaine. The transaction took place in the casino's parking lot. As I have mentioned prior and if you were paying attention, we chose the casino because the parking lot had good cameras for better surveillance. We soon found, every time Sammy would show up for a delivery, he was never alone. Either someone would ride with him or follow in a separate vehicle.

After that first purchase, Sammy became comfortable with me and I would call him directly and order cocaine. On one particular delivery, we made arrangements for me to purchase one pound of cocaine. The agreement was to meet in the casino parking lot and complete the transaction.

I arrived prior to the agreed time. My surveillance team had set up in their vehicles blending in among all the other vehicles in the parking lot. A couple of our agents were inside the security office, monitoring the transaction through the video cameras.

I intentionally parked my undercover vehicle at a location I knew the surveillance team in the video room would have a better view of the transaction. Sammy arrived and called me on my cell phone. I told him where I was parked and invited him to park next to me. Sammy parked his Camaro to the right of me and climbed into the front passenger side of my vehicle. As expected, Sammy was not alone, he was followed by an associate of his whom I had not met and he too parked his vehicle directly in front of my vehicle. The associate got out and opened the hood of his pickup truck. Pointing to this individual, I asked Sammy who that person was. He said not to worry he was with him. He went on to say that he opened the hood of the truck to block the view of any surveillance cameras. I worried for a moment that Sammy may ask to do the transaction at a different location if he was worried about cameras.

As I may have mentioned before hardly any undercover drug transaction go as planned. During a buy/walk briefing we try to come up with different scenarios of "what ifs" in case a plan changes. On this particular buy/ walk we were hoping to keep the transaction at the casino so any persons involved could be identified and most importantly the safety factor of everyone involved, especially 'moi'.

While seated in the passenger seat of my UC vehicle, Sammy removed a cellophane package from inside his shirt and handed it to me. As I was inspecting the package containing the white powdery cocaine the third unexpected bad guy who had parked in front of me, opened the rear passenger door, and sat in the back seat. I was seated on the driver's side and kind of shifted so I could see this new visitor. Sammy introduced him to me as "Tony"; I returned the greeting and remained seated at an angle so I could keep an eye on him and Sammy. I also knew we had a video recorder inside the cab of my Suburban. The video camera was situated where it could record the transaction and it was running, or at least I had hoped it was.

I handed Sammy the buy money I kept in a paper sack. Sammy took the money ($11,000) out of the bag and commenced to counting. I glanced over at Tony and he had both hands in front of him covering what I saw to be a chrome plated firearm. I began to get a bit nervous with all kinds of scenarios running through my head. I forced myself to remain calm (I was getting pretty good about that) until Sammy finished counting the money.

After counted the money Sammy said it was good and placed the bundle of money in his shirt. Tony got out of the back seat and went to his vehicle. I was relieved he left. Sammy appeared happy the deal went well and told me to call him directly if I needed any more. I told him I would need more soon and I would call.

After departing the casino parking lot, I was certainly relieved and elated at the same time. The adrenaline was rushing through me; I was beginning to like this kind of high. I drove around the city for a little bit watching my rear view mirrors to be certain no one was following me. After I arrived at the task force, my adrenaline level was at an all-time high. I turned in the package of cocaine and it was tested (chemically of course) and weighed. The video camera was removed from the UC vehicle and we watched it on the monitor. It turned out to be an excellent video. It captured the cocaine and money handover. It also captured part of Tony in the back seat.

The weekend that followed, on a Sunday, I was surprised to get a call from Tony. He asked if I was going to the horse races south of town. I told him I had not planned on it and he said to pick him up because he wanted to go. I could feel my heart pumping as the adrenaline began rushing through my veins. I recall thinking either I am in good with this organization or it's a set up and I was going to wind up buried in the dessert.

I immediately called my boss, the task force commander, and told him about the call I just received. The commander (Boss) asked if I felt comfortable about doing this and of course I was not going to say no. I told him I was comfortable and this is my chance to get in deeper with these people. He agreed and told me he would call me back so he could get a team together to conduct surveillance.

A short time later, Boss called me and again asked if I was comfortable in going. *"yes Boss, no worries. Let's get going"* I told him. I called Tony back and told him to give me some time to get into town (I was already in town but needed time to get the team ready and make an operational plan). Tony gave me his home address and told me to pick him up when I got into town.

The race track is located south of town and a private horse race was held every other Sunday. A great many of the people that attend are involved in the drug trade. I wanted to go so I could be seen with a known trafficker therefore they would think I was one of them as well. The word would certainly get out about me being with Tony and I was purchasing cocaine.

The surveillance team got set up and drove to the location. They, the surveillance team, however could not get into the race track area so they had to watch from a great distance away. I drove to the address provided to me by Tony. Tony came out and got into my truck. He greeted me and asked if I had ever been to the horse races.

I must add, all the conversation with these people is in Spanish. Most of the people involved are from Mexico or have ties in Mexico. That is one of the reasons the surveillance team could not inter the race track. They would stick out. Am I profiling you ask? Yes, the agents were white (Ok, "non-Hispanic") and certainly would not fit in to that type of crowd. It is what it is. I had hoped they were a little closer in case I needed assistance.

On our drive to the race track, Tony said to me, the reason he sat behind us during my last transaction with Sammy, he was supposed to shoot me first if any cops showed up or was seen in the area. After the hairs in the back of my neck stood up, I remember thinking *"thank God this was a buy/walk"*.

We arrived at the track. As we entered the private property crossing over cattle guards and drove up to a gate attendant, a plump Mexican woman. I was getting ready to pay the entrance fee when the woman saw Tony and greeted him. They exchanged a few words and she told me to drive on in. Tony said they usually charge to enter the property but they won't charge him. I noticed the race track was a straight-a-way track with the racing gates on the far end. There were already several trucks with horse trailers at the location. Tony said it was still early and soon the place would be packed. He went on to say at times there is a band on the location because there is a party after the races. He directed me to park in front of the track.

After parking, Tony and I walked around and it seemed like everyone knew him. He would introduce me as his friend Jimmy. I always kept in the back of my mind what if someone would recognize me or what if someone was there from south Texas where I had been a police officer for many years. That may be a long shot but one never knows. I slowly began to get comfortable. Some of the people I was introduced to, had ice chest with beer. We were offered beer and I accepted it. Hey dear readers, I have to do what I must to make this case. Don't judge me.

I tried to stay in contact with the surveillance team by text messages. At times I would receive calls from the team members to check on my status and I would speak to them as if I was talking to ranch hands or family members. They knew I was drinking cold beers in that hot desert sun while they were a ways off in the heat with no cold beer. I really felt their pain (not really). Someone had to do it. Again, no judging me.

The purpose for me being there seemed to work out. I was seen with Tony, a known trafficker of cocaine. Tony talked to me a little about his back ground. He mentioned he had worked for some of the big cartels in Mexico as a hit man. He mentioned at one point he was at a ranch in Mexico and had seen barrels of chemical acids where bodies were being disposed of. How true that was, I did not know. I put that in a report anyway.

One of the person's I was introduced by Tony became one of the biggest targets of this operation. Ramon. (Not his real name).

Ramon was a local so called business man that involved himself in the cocaine trade. He had been a major supplier of cocaine in southeast New Mexico and West Texas. Many of the suspects I had been purchasing cocaine from, were being supplied by Ramon. When I first was introduced to him by Tony, Ramon was told I purchased large amounts of cocaine and transport it to clients I supposedly had in north Texas. At the race track Ramon told me he would like to do business with me and for me not to call anyone else for my supply. I was glad to hear that.

As time went on, I enlisted the help of a female agent I will call Kat (readers, if you were paying attention, I already mentioned Kat on another page). Often Kat and I visited Ramon at his place of business. She would go with me as "my niece". While I was discussing business with Ramon, Kat would be on her cell phone texting as most young girls did. Except she would be sending messages to the surveillance team such as license plate numbers and names. At times, Ramon's wife would begin conversation with Kat as well.

Ramon and I, in my undercover role, became friends. He would invite me to his house on several occasion for parties and drug transaction. On a couple occasion I brought other UC agents to the house that played the part as either a nephew or employee. Ramon seemed to trust me as I purchased more cocaine from him. His children would refer to me as 'Tio Jimmy' (uncle).

One evening an undercover agent from another task force and I went to Ramon's house to purchase a pound of cocaine. I introduced the undercover as my nephew. Ramon invited us in. He took us around the house showing us photos of his race horses he had hanging in various rooms. We went to the dining table and sat. Next to the dining room was the living room and several children were in there watching television. We sat at the kitchen table and Ramon brought out a large clear plastic bag containing cocaine and placed it on the table. I remembered feeling uncomfortable as we were in full view of the children. I asked Ramon if we should be doing this deal in front of the children. He said it was alright and there was no problem. He began scooping the powder cocaine from the bag he had into another bag that was on a scale. One of his sons about five or six years of age came to the table to see him weigh the cocaine. I was thinking to myself how sad I was for these kids having to see this and they thinking I was like their father.

Several large amounts of cocaine were purchased from Ramon and we thought it was time to move up the ladder and purchase from a different source.

I did get to spend a lot of time with Ramon and his family as an undercover. I knew one day he and whoever else involved were going to prison at some point and I was glad for that.

•

It was during this same operation where Ramon introduced me to another heavy dealer. This person, I will call Abe. Abe lived on a little ranch south of town and he too was involved in the cocaine and horse racing business. When I was introduced to him, he immediately became comfortable with me coming around. I would show up unannounced at times. The surveillance team had to keep watch from a distance as well because of the location and Abe's neighbors were known to keep watch if any strange vehicles or persons were seen in the area.

One day, I arrived at Abe's residence to pick up three ounces of cocaine. I knocked on the trailer door and was met by an unidentified Mexican male subject. I asked for Abe and was told that he was not in and would return shortly. This person invited me in and said I was welcomed to wait. As I walked in, I noticed three other Hispanic subjects sitting around the kitchen table. The person that let me in identified himself to me as Chapo.

Chapo told me I could wait in the living room or in the Kitchen with the others. Chapo appeared to be drunk or high at the time. I decided to go to the kitchen where the others were sitting and noticed they were smoking what they called 'foilies'. This was done by smoothing out a piece of aluminum foil about 12 inches square. They then would moisten the top part with either water or some kind of alcohol drink. In this case it was Vodka. They then sprinkle powder cocaine on the foil, covering it evenly. With a straw or glass pipe in their mouth they would hold up the piece of foil in one hand and with the other hand holding a lighter, they then inhale the smoke or fumes that came off the foil.

As I stood there talking to them, they passed the foil paper around. I was asked if I wanted some and declined. They were smoking, and drinking the different kinds of liquor that was on the table.

Chapo, seemed to be getting higher or drunk (maybe both) as the moment went on. I began to worry about my surveillance team not hearing from me or being able to visually observe me. I mentioned to these people that I was in the horse training business and I wanted to go check on the horses in the pens outside. Chapo said he would take me out to see them. My main purpose was to be seen outside by the surveillance team so that they would know I was ok.

Chapo and I went out to the corrals and looked at the horses. He began asking questions as to how I met Abe. I told him I was Ramon's friend. Chapo mentioned to me that they were all friends from Mexico and all had worked for different cartels.

While we were outside, I unexpectedly, received a phone call from a female analyst I knew that worked for the Feds as an analyst. She was contacted by the surveillance team and told to call me on my cell phone and act like she was my wife. The surveillance team wanted to know what my status was since they could not hear my conversation. The transmitter I was wearing in my pocket was not working. As I was speaking to the analyst I acted like she was my wife and told her I was fine and would be home soon. I was waiting for my friend to arrive to pick up something. She relayed the message to the surveillance team. During the course of this operation, she called or text me to be sure I was alright.

Chapo and I went back in the house where he went back to smoking the foilies. The house we were in was filling with cocaine induced fumes. All the windows and doors were shut. I could feel myself get a bit light headed so I made excuses to go outside for fresh air and the benefit of the surveillance team.

Once back inside, Chapo and I were in the living room and he began to get loud. He began telling me that the drug task force and the state police were there about two weeks prior to conduct a search warrant. He said they had searched the house and had not found the gun he had hidden. Chapo pulled out a loaded 45 automatic. He bragged that while searching the residence they did not find the weapon that was hidden in the recliner where he was seated. My spider senses began going off. This man was higher than a kite, holding a loaded 45, waving it around and claimed to work for the cartel. Something had to change here and quickly.

I asked Chapo if I could see the gun because I might want to purchase it. He handed me the gun while he was still somewhat irate because of the search warrant. I must add here, I was involved in in that very same search warrant he spoke about, two weeks prior. I assisted in searching the barn on the property and was wearing my Balaclava (hood/mask) so I was not recognized. During my search, I found a pound of cocaine hidden in the horse feed barrel.

As I took the gun from Chapo, immediately removed the magazine and placed it on a table next to me. I ejected the round from the chamber and pretended to admire the weapon. All the while I was telling Chapo how nice the gun was. I asked him if he would sell it to me. I did not want this idiot to have a loaded weapon especially while I was there. When Chapo declined to sell me the weapon, I laid it next to me on the coffee table, deliberately not reinserting the magazine. Quickly I changed the subject so he would not get the gun back.

Shortly after Abe arrived and greeted me. I told him what I wanted and got my three ounces of cocaine. With the cocaine in possession, I quickly got the hell out. I have never felt more relief as when I got out of there.

I met up with the surveillance team at a different location to hand them the acquired cocaine and I noticed my hands and legs were shaking as the adrenaline was subsiding from my body.

Operation Los Amigos ended with the arrest of multiple suspects, seizures of large amount of narcotics and all of our agents got to return to their families safely.

It was reported to me during one of my, later UC purchases from another bad guy that Ramon was killed in Mexico because of his association with me "Jimmy".

•

There was never any honor among thieves as they say. Often times while on the Los Amigos operation, Tony would introduce me to other suppliers and tell me not to say anything to Carlos or Ramon. He wanted to keep the money he made on any deal all to himself. He made several boast about working for different cartels in Mexico which was later confirmed.

Outlaw Motorcycle Gangs (OMGs)

I mentioned earlier in this book about meeting and hanging out and with members of a certain outlaw motorcycle gang. Just to be clear, I was not trying to work on any particular person or member of this OMG. It was by chance that I met them during the course of my work as an undercover. As time went on and I got to attend functions or just be around them whenever possible, I always maintained that it was good for my reputation as a supposedly bad guy to be seen with the OMGs.

This group I speak about is one of the top 5 one percenter (1%) outlaw motorcycle gang in the nation. They are indeed many outlaw bikers that consider themselves 1%s. One percenters are not sanctioned by the American Motorcyclist Association and do not follow AMA rules. That is what the 1% indicates.

In the capacity I was working as, I wanted to be seen around the OMG by any potential drug client. It was good for business as they say. I figured if the drug dealers see me around these bikers I must be ok. I did get to meet with some other members of other OMGs but as I said I wasn't trying to work on anyone one of them in particular. I did find out later, after I left or came out (not the closet) that my photo was being passed around among the bikers. It was after I worked an operation at a local spice shop. My picture was taken as soon as I walked through the door at this particular shop to purchase spice "incense". I was told by reliable sources I was not very well thought of at this point by this group.

I must say though, and not to give any praise to anyone OMG member because many are still and have been involved with organized criminal activity, but many of the patched members I had contact with, were working class people. Many of them had families and are former veterans. I know some of you will say," yea, but they are still criminals anyway". Well perhaps, we do the best we can. I guess we can claim some politicians may be considered 1 percenters but I don't want to piss off any OMGs for comparing them to politicians.

I could probably write an entire book on the Outlaw Motorcycle Gangs but I'll leave it for another time.

●

I enjoyed being an undercover agent. You might say it was a passion. Everyone I had the pleasure of working with truly believed in what they were doing. In either of my time with the Lea County Drug Task Force and the Pecos Valley Drug Task Force, I never saw or felt there was any type of inappropriate conduct among the agents. Yes, among ourselves, there were many pranks but nothing that would jeopardize the integrity of a case or the oath we took as law enforcement officers.

Many agents I have met and spoke too would get frustrated as much as I did with all the policies and restrictions we as a task force, had to comply with. There were several instances during the course of an investigation; we encountered certain situations where we felt our hands tied. The higher level of government we were involved with, the higher bureaucracy we had to contend with. On many occasion, I would ask myself, does the government really wanted to win a war on drugs? Even within the judicial system, we as law enforcement officers would encounter the most frustration. Going to court on what we would believe to be an open and shut case. With video and audio evidence, you would think the trial would be a done deal. That was not always the case. Many of us have been attacked by defense attorneys as to our integrity. I know all about "due process" and every one has the right to a fair trial. Thus the reason for my frustration. I wanted to put the bad guys in jail and move on to the next operation. The prosecutors, both federal and state level were some of the hardest working, underpaid, truly unrecognized professionals I have had the pleasure of working with.

Some of my friends and family that knew what I was doing for a living would mention they envied me for working undercover and hanging out at the bars living a double life. They would ask questions about what it was like. My answer to them was it is not all that glamorous. It was not like the movies or anything they have seen on television. After a while it became stressful for me. I got to the point where I would look around for familiar faces of bad guys anywhere I would go. I still by habit, look for potential clients when I walk into a place. To this day, if I am out at a place of business, I look at people and think to myself "is this person involved in something or I bet I can buy something from this person". It became second nature for me to look at a person in the way they conduct themselves.

It is a common misconception by the bad guys and many of the public that, If we were ever asked if we are the police we have to tell them the truth. Not only no, but HELL NO. It is our job as undercover agents to make these people believe we are bad guys just like they are. In many of the cases upon first meeting a bad guy they will ask if you are POLICE. They too believe that police cannot lie to them. Surprise! You are going to jail. The low level dealers are the ones that usually believe that. I do not recall ever been asked by any of the suppliers involved in the sales of higher quantity of narcotics.

Everyone I have worked alongside or met during an operation whether it was local, state or federal, are indeed true professionals that I trusted with my life. I did not trust leaving my undercover vehicle or my office unsecured around them at any given time, but I trusted them with my life. These agents spent countless of hours away from their families to do what most will not or what many only dreamed of doing. I say to them, I apologize about me having to act like I was enjoying myself while on an undercover operation and you were on surveillance in the hot summer sun or in the cold winter nights. Thank you for being there.

I also give my sincere thanks to the officers and agents of local, state and federal agencies I had the pleasure of meeting and working alongside throughout my career. Unfortunately I cannot name anyone as there are many. You know who you are. God Bless and watch over you.

Watch your 6

I take this opportunity to thank my daughters, Jackie, Sarah and Bobbie Lynn and to my son Patrick, for enduring and understanding the times I had to be away from you. There was never a day I did not think of you. Your thoughts and prayers are what kept me safe. I cannot end without thanking my mother Julie Willis who provided me lots of prayers for my safety, encouragement and strength.

Der Komerad

Wenn einor von uns müde wird, der andere für ihn wacht
Wenn einor von uns zweifein will, der andere gläubig lacht
Wenn einor von uns fallen solit, der andere steht für zwei
Denn jedem kämper gibt ein Gott den kameraden bei

Herybert Menzel

If one of gets tired, the other one is watching out for two
If one of us thinks he didn't do the right thing. The other one says believe
in it
If one of us gets killed, the other one stands for two, because God gives
every soldier a comrade

Herybert Menzel

Submitted by **Per M Griebler** MSgt (Ret) German Army – Nov 1998 to
Aug 2011. Mechanized Infantry Tank Commander and Military Police. 2
deployments to Kosovo 2004 and 2009 with deployments in Afghanistan
in 2005.

MSgt Griebler is also the author of the book **'13 Years of Service'**.

Job 28:28

And to man he said, Behold, the fear of the Lord that is wisdom: and to depart from evil is understanding

Submitted by **James Coonrod** – United States Marine Corps 1966 to 1970: Vietnam 1967-1969

Joshua 24:15

And if it seem evil unto you to serve the Lord, choose you this day whom ye will serve; whether the gods which your fathers served that were on the other side of the flood, or the gods of the Amorites, in whose land ye dwell: but as for me and my house, we will serve the Lord.

Submitted by **David Kemp** United Stated Marine Corps 1992 to 1996, MOS 6531 (Aviation Ordinance) HMLA 367 and HMLA 369 "The Gunfighters"

Psalm 46:10

Be still, and know that I am God

Submitted by; **Tim G Mehl**
US Navy – USS Richard S Edwards (DD-950), Vietnam 1972
El Paso Police Department (24 years-retired)

"Be Safe"

Submitted by, **Anthony Budrow**
Lea County Sheriff's Department
US Army Reserve 85/86
US Air Force 1986-1990

Ephesians 6:10

"A final word: Be strong in the Lord and in his mighty power. Put on all of Gods armor so that you will be able to stand firm against all strategies of the devil".

"I won't be wronged, I won't be insulted and I won't be laid a hand on. I don't do these things to other people and I require the same from them".

John Wayne as JB Books – The Shootist

Submitted by Carroll Caudill
Eddy County Sheriff Department (Ret)
US Army 1983-1993 Military Police

"Working narcotics, teaches you how not to be a police officer"
Lyon Newman
Eddy County New Mexico SO (retired)